# PRAISE FOR INSIDE CEO SUCCESSION

*"While* Inside CEO Succession *contains a very useful analysis of key steps boards can use to create a successful process, what I found to be invaluable were the examples of successful and failed succession programs cited by the authors. These stories illustrated topics that are rarely discussed in this context. Personal emotions, psychological challenges, organizational culture, and the critical partnership between the board and the CEO can all influence the succession process. These insights, based on decades of experience on the part of authors Tom Saporito and Paul Winum, are the book's greatest strength."*

—Freeman A. Hrabowski, III, president, University of Maryland, Baltimore County; named by *Time Magazine* as one of the Top 100 most influential people in the world for 2012; director, McCormick & Company, Baltimore Equitable Society, and the Alfred P. Sloan Foundation

*"Tom Saporito and Paul Winum's new book on CEO succession is a treasure trove of practical advice and is a must-read for any company thinking about building a solid path to its future leadership. The book is richly detailed with solid research and real world examples and it offers a compelling conceptual framework and step by step process for all aspects of CEO succession and transition. Given the importance of this topic and the shortage of literature in this field, there's no doubt that Tom and Paul's groundbreaking book will become the standard reference for all Boards that are grappling with the question of CEO succession."*

—Chip Perry, president and CEO, AutoTrader.com

"Inside CEO Succession *is chock full of insights on a critical subject for today's boards and executive teams. Tom Saporito and Paul Winum know that succession planning is more than simply a leadership transition. In this book, they capture its essence as a living, breathing, ongoing process which directly impacts corporate success and failure."*
—Paul Charron, chairman of the board, Campbell Soup Company; former CEO, Liz Claiborne Inc.

"Inside CEO Succession *provides a unique, nuanced insight into psychological and emotional aspects involved in succession that many boards fail to recognize. Particularly insightful are the authors' emphases on the disciplined process needed during pre- and post-selection transition, succession as a selection of CEO and senior team, and the importance of a board's ability to evaluate leadership attributes required for changing future market and business. The book offers practical steps to a successful CEO transition in an environment of economic uncertainty, regulation complexity, ever-quickening technology shifts, and broadening groups of stakeholders."*
—Deven Sharma, former CEO, Standard and Poors

*"Chief executive succession is more art than science, more a board mindset than a process. By clearly demonstrating why CEO succession needs to be more board-driven than CEO-driven, Tom Saporito and Paul Winum make an important contribution toward how companies can better manage this important transition."*
—Fred Hassan, managing director–healthcare, Warburg Pincus; chairman, Bausch and Lomb; former chairman and CEO, Schering Plough; director, Time Warner and Avon

*"Having worked with RHR for many years and seeing them in action inside our companies, it is no surprise to me that Paul Winum and Tom Saporito have penned an outstanding guide for any director seeking insight into their most important job—ensuring consistent, strong leadership . Management teams and companies are constantly evolving and companies with great management over the long term don't just get lucky, they carefully plan. This book covers the complete life cycle of leadership change and is a must-read for any director who aspires to embody board-level best practices."*

—Mark Jennings, managing partner and founder,
Generation Partners; chairman of the board of
trustees, Post University; former director,
Virtual Radiologic Corporation,
inVentiv Health, MedVance Institute, and
Agility Recovery Solutions

*"Saporito and Winum have written a straightforward, insightful and extremely valuable book that all boards and CEOs should read—and follow. Their collective professional experience and the nearly 70 years of RHR's leadership in the field of executive selection, development and effectiveness make this work the 'gold standard' for CEO succession. As they clearly articulate—and as the historical data supports—getting this wrong has significant negative consequences for business and all of the stakeholders."*

—Ned Guillet, former senior vice president,
The Gillette Company

"*The hallmark of successful CEO succession is to identify the challenges ahead for the corporation—how the operating and competitive environments will change—and choose the right leader who has experience, knowledge and skills to lead the organization in that new environment.* Inside CEO Succession *provides the unique perspectives and experiences of Tom Saporito and Paul Winum, who have 'walked the walk' in this critical area of corporate leadership."*
—C. Manly Molpus, former president and CEO,
Grocery Manufacturers Association; director,
SPAR Group; CPG advisory board, Procurian


"*Tom Saporito and Paul Winum, two of the superlative senior consultants from the legendary RHR International consulting firm, have produced a comprehensive and understandable guide that makes the mysterious, dangerous, and challenging work of transition management possible for boards and leadership teams to do well together. It is full of terrific case material, specific advice about the necessary components of a corporate program, and practical wisdom for leaders and consultants. Succession management is an extraordinarily critical aspect of the work of corporate governance members. It is full of ambiguity, anxiety, and the constant threat of failure. Saporito, Winum, and the RHR methodology would help virtually every firm navigate these processes more successfully."*
—Richard R. Kilburg, Ph.D., author of *Executive Coaching, Executive Wisdom,* and *Virtuous Leaders,* among other books and articles on leadership and management

# INSIDE CEO
# SUCCESSION

# INSIDE CEO SUCCESSION

## THE ESSENTIAL GUIDE TO LEADERSHIP TRANSITION

TOM SAPORITO
& PAUL WINUM

John Wiley & Sons Canada, Ltd.

**Library of Congress Cataloging-in-Publication Data**

Thomas J. Saporito
   Inside CEO succession : the essential guide to leadership transition / by Thomas J. Saporito and Paul Winum.
      p. cm.
   Includes bibliographical references and index.
   ISBN 978-1-118-20321-7 (cloth)
   1.   Executive succession. 2.   Chief executive officers  3.   Directors of corporations. 4.   Executives—Selection and appointment. 5.   Management. I. Winum, Paul   II. Title.
   HD38.2.W563 2012
   658.4'0711--dc23

                                                                              2012017198

978-1-118-21802-0 (ebk); 978-1-118-21801-3 (ebk); 978-1-118-21803-7 (ebk)

**Production Credits**
Cover design: Adrian So
Typesetting: Thomson Digital
Cover image: Thinkstock
Printer: Courier

**Author Photos**
Photo of Thomas J. Saporito: Paladino Photography
Photo of Paul Winum: Santa Barbara Photography

**Editorial Credits**
Executive editor: Don Loney
Managing editor: Alison Maclean
Production editor: Jeremy Hanson-Finger

Printed in the United States of America

2 3 4 5 COU 16 15 14 13 12

# CONTENTS

# ACKNOWLEDGMENTS

While one or two persons might have their names printed on the cover, the truth is that legions of people are involved in the publication of a book from concept through distribution. This volume is no exception and we would like to acknowledge their efforts. To name all of the individuals who have touched our careers and our practices would take more pages than reasonable. For that reason, we have taken the liberty of departing from the usual practice and have listed our contributors in groups, thereby ensuring that no one's effort is slighted by omission.

First of all, the concepts in this book would never have been developed without the clients of RHR International. Each and every CEO succession situation is unique, and working with a variety of CEOs, board members, senior teams and candidates in companies of all sizes have given the firm the opportunity to see the process unfold in many different ways. Some were successful, some were not. It was these real life situations that allowed us to constantly refine our own model, applying the best practices of the time, but always modifying and evolving our views of what worked and what did not. It is the culmination of all those years of practical experience with some very unique individuals that fills the following pages. We believe the fact that many of our earliest clients are still with us testifies to the trust they have in us as advisors. Many of these relationships have evolved over the years from business associations into close personal friendships.

With the clients providing the challenges, it was the consultants of RHR International, past and present, who were called on to provide the solutions. Not only did they each have the experience, the business acumen and the training necessary to address CEO succession issues, each generation has had the invaluable ability to draw on the knowledge and wisdom of those who came before. This open melding of the minds in classrooms, offices, restaurants, airports and even the occasional golf course strengthens our practice with each and every conversation. Wherever we are, we talk shop . . . a lot! And gems of knowledge are often uncovered in the most casual of settings. Yes, the discussions can get heated, but it is in the fires of debate that the truth is revealed. While it is never billed back to a client, the consultants of RHR never stop observing, wondering, discussing and evolving our service areas. It has been this way since our founding approximately 70 years ago, and it is our fervent wish that it will always be so.

Throughout the years, RHR International has built a reputation for groundbreaking research on our core service areas—backing up experience, observation and intuition with solid data. Some studies validated what we had come to believe, others challenged us to step back and take another look and purposefully move in a new direction. Without the dedication of our research teams throughout the years, this vital conduit of knowledge and wisdom would have been lost to us. Equally important, if not more so, are the directors, chief executive officers and other senior executives who have given most generously of their most precious commodity—time. They have contributed to the wealth of knowledge on management best practices by granting us interviews and answering the surveys that gave us the raw data for our studies. Without this gift, none of it—the research, the analysis, the creation of new intervention programs, the practical application to the benefit of organizations worldwide—would have been possible.

In the last three years, we have compiled the latest information gathered from and by the groups listed above. The result is this book. We believe it is the state-of-the-art resource for those organizations that could benefit from a grounding in the most up to date information on CEO succession possible. Is it the Bible on the topic? Of course not: each business is unique, each past and future chief executive will have behaviors and abilities that must be assessed and evaluated in light of the organization's current needs and strategic goals. However, thanks to the dedication and efforts of RHR International's clients, consultants, researchers and study participants, you are unlikely to find a more comprehensive work on the topic of CEO succession on bookshelves today.

We deeply appreciate all the efforts of our fellow contributors, even if there was no room on the cover for your names.

# FOREWORD

CEO succession planning is arguably the most important responsibility of a board of directors. A wise succession choice can lead to a meaningful value creation story for all stakeholders, while a poor choice can render just the opposite effect. Given the relative importance of this board responsibility, I have found it surprising that there is a paucity of consistent best practice on this front.

For the better part of two decades, I have experienced every facet of succession planning in my capacity as student, participant, and practitioner. I have been a candidate for succession who has not been chosen and one who has been selected to succeed. I have been responsible for shepherding the CEO succession process for four boards of directors—one corporate and three, large not-for-profit organizations. And I have culminated my experience administering to my own succession, identifying and preparing my successor, and transitioning my leadership to the incoming CEO.

Through all of my succession experiences and that of my colleagues, I have observed that the opportunities for improvement in the process have been more pronounced than the elements that have been well managed.

Fortunately, Tom Saporito and Paul Winum of RHR International have crafted this important guide to effective leadership transition. I have known Tom and Paul for over a decade, during which time they have ably assisted the organizations that I have been associated with on this front in both the corporate and not-for-profit sectors. In particular, they capably supported the leadership development and transition process as I managed within and retired from Campbell Soup Company as president and CEO.

Through a powerful combination of deep study of this space, vast experience in helping organizations navigate the challenges resident in the succession process, and years of practice and training in the field of psychology, the RHR team has developed a compelling perspective—a precise collection of best practices in succession planning as a partnership between the board and the CEO.

Leveraging many of the elements of these practices at Campbell, we were able to advance a quality succession process that enabled us to retain and develop our key talent, maintain and, in fact, enhance our strategic heading, and sustain a world class, high employee engagement culture.

More specifically, in this work, Tom and Paul advance a thoughtfully compelling case around the importance of getting the CEO succession formula right—a case anchored in solid thinking and brought to life with real-world examples. Once the essence of the challenge is made crystal clear at the onset of this book, a rich dialogue ensues over the 10 key dimensions of effective succession planning, providing a very helpful, end-to-end view of the entire process.

The authors establish a clear articulation of board ownership, involvement, and oversight and define the essentials of a well-orchestrated planning approach between board and CEO—elements that lead to the ultimate selection of a CEO and culminate in a process for proactively managing the post-selection transition.

In my study and experience, the knowledge and wisdom captured in the pages of this work is second-to-none on the subject of CEO succession. The approach advanced by Tom and Paul takes the mystery out of the process, creates a common platform around which directors can find consensus, and brings a refreshing clarity to the subject.

Leveraging this guide as a tool, any board can materially improve the productivity of its leadership transition process. I heartily recommend it.

Douglas R. Conant
Retired President, CEO, and Director
Campbell Soup Company

# INTRODUCTION

The business environment has undergone significant transformation over the past several decades—progressing from the relative simplicity of commerce in the mid-twentieth century, to the market expansions and consolidations of the 1980s and 1990s, to the global interconnectedness of our current era.

These volatile and chaotic times are demanding more from boards and company leaders than at any other time in history and, to ensure the continuity of business, the selection and transitioning of a company's CEO has been elevated to the most important undertaking an organization can engage in.

With the complexities involved in selecting and transitioning the chief executive increasing with each passing decade, the mindset of the past and the methods used then are, in many ways, inadequate for ensuring success in today's business climate. We have all seen the results of this insufficiency played out too often in the business press with news of companies struggling to survive failed leadership.

Public scrutiny of business and management has certainly accentuated the issue and shareholders have become acutely aware of the need for greater discipline in CEO succession planning. Change in a company's management is now one of the most important areas for investors to follow. Shareholders are also beginning to realize—especially given the high-profile departures and dismissals of CEOs—a greater need for corporate governance and that CEO succession planning depends, in large part, on an established process originating at the board level.

Many boards today are quite conscious of the growing demand and their obligation. They are a) more keenly aware of the need for CEO succession planning than their predecessors, and b) more prepared, with succession plans and processes firmly in place. However, even with all this awareness and preparedness, directors are still beleaguered, to varying degrees, by the relational dynamics and personal emotions that attend every step of the succession planning process—from candidate development, to final selection, to the transfer of power, to the integration of the new CEO.

In our years of experience, we have concluded that addressing and managing the psychological forces and organizational dynamics are what truly defines best practice and success in CEO succession planning. Yet, there is very little support and insight offered to companies on how to best undertake succession planning *and* navigate the emotions that attend every step of the process.

*Inside CEO Succession* offers that very guidance. We take you inside the essential steps required to establish a best practice in succession planning, inside the relational dynamics among board members and between the board and the CEO, and inside the personal emotions that sway and influence even the most experienced executives—an often-overlooked aspect of the success or failure of the succession process.

Another critical distinction of our practice, illustrated throughout this book, is our belief that CEO succession is more than a board's responsibility. Although the board is accountable for the process, we strongly believe that there must be a partnership between board and CEO—a partnership built on personal authenticity and trust. Best practice can only be achieved when board and CEO reach an understanding of involvement—a division of labor orchestrated by the board and adhered to by both parties.

*Inside CEO Succession* is the culmination of approximately 70 years of providing expert counsel to boards and management on how to best manage the succession planning process and ensure the substance and effectiveness of its leadership. We have gained as much as we have given. Fundamental to our experience is the invaluable education we have received from our clients over the years—from board members, to CEOs, to future leaders—insightful lessons shared within these chapters.

Over the past five years, our firm RHR International has undertaken an extensive program of primary research, annually surveying hundreds of board members of top companies across a variety of industries on their views on succession planning. We have conducted in-depth interviews with board chairs and lead directors to understand their approach to succession planning and what factors contribute to both good and poor outcomes—also shared in the pages that follow.

Additionally, and as a finger on the pulse of contemporary business, we present examples of high-profile companies, pulled directly out of today's business press, illustrating both success and failure in the succession and transitioning of leadership.

*Inside CEO Succession* is a unique mixture of business experience and educational training: a blend of process and perception. While our 10 Key Dimensions of Succession Planning provide an essential guide for establishing a best practice in succession planning, our experiences as doctoral-level psychologists grounds us in assessing and addressing the social-psychological factors of ego, role-relationships, power, and emotion associated with relinquishing leadership, preparing successors, and ceding power and authority to others.

If properly attended to and thoughtfully executed, CEO succession can offer a company far more than the transitioning of its top leader. CEO succession can enable companies to envision new opportunities for growth, to realign and strengthen processes and systems throughout the enterprise, and propel companies to greater results in the service of their missions.

Thomas J. Saporito
Paul Winum

# PART I

# Why CEO Succession Is More Critical than Ever

CEO succession is more than an important issue; it is fundamental to a company's sustained success. The disconnect between how important this issue is and the willingness of boards to tackle it can be attributed to the fact that it is a time-consuming process and many board members are ill-prepared to manage it.

Moreover, the psychological forces and organizational dynamics involving such issues as power, ego, legacy, and personal agendas have as much influence on the process as objective data, procedures, and timelines.

For the sake of business continuity and a company's sustained effectiveness, there are no reasons to ignore or give brief and inconsiderate attention to the selection and transitioning of a company's leadership. History has shown that a firm's capital and assets are not the ultimate determinants of its success or failure, but rather the firm's individuals who govern, lead, manage, and deploy those resources.

# From Checkers to 3-D Chess

# 1

*"Business is a highly-charged and ever-changing environment. Businesses strive to evolve so they can maintain their fitness to compete. CEO succession has to start with, and run in parallel to, the incumbent's role if a business is to have any hope of keeping up momentum. Missing this nuance means it is doomed to making transitional decisions that could have a negative impact on the future."*
—James P. Hackett, CEO and
president of Steelcase, Inc.

It is very difficult for a leader—any leader—to step down and hand over the reins of their company to someone else. Human nature being what it is, power is a most difficult force to surrender to another. Those who aspire to positions of leadership are ambitious, highly motivated, and exceedingly driven individuals, so any activity involving the interplay of personalities, emotions, ego, and legacy is going to present relational obstacles when planning and executing the transition from one chief executive to another. Given the ever-present undercurrent of these powerful social and psychological forces, CEO succession will always prove a most difficult reality for many CEOs to gracefully accept, and is one of the most challenging activities for a board of directors to oversee.

What has added to the complexity of CEO succession planning over the years are the demands of a rapidly changing and highly competitive business environment. The succession process itself, and the ramifications of transitional decisions, were far less complicated and consequential sixty-seven years ago when RHR International began advising and guiding companies in their CEO succession planning. The business environment then was far simpler when compared to the speed, complexity and uncertainty of the business world we live and work in today.

Yet with all that has changed over the years in the conduct of business, the discipline of succession planning has not kept pace and advanced accordingly. The hesitant mindset of CEOs and boards—combined with the displacement of the critical tasks related to succession planning by the urgent matters of the day—have repeatedly proven detrimental to continuity of leadership and growth of many companies.

## A SIMPLE, MORE PREDICTABLE WORLD

The years following World War II ushered in an economic boom and an end to the Great Depression. The post-war period also set in motion an explosion in consumer purchasing power, fueled by credit cards, shopping centers, the "golden age" of television, and the interstate highway system. AT&T was everyone's phone company, and the Big Three were the only three in North America.

Conducting business in the 1950s, 60s, and 70s was analogous to a game of checkers. Winning was simply a matter of staying one or two steps ahead of competition. Though every move had the potential to bring about a variety of counter-moves, the CEOs of many of the *Fortune* 500 companies at the time could comprehend the entire playing board at once and make short- and long-term decisions with a high degree of confidence.

The business environment was straightforward and, to a certain degree, predictable. Companies engaged in commerce primarily in their own country, encountered known competitors, served traditional market segments, and offered limited product choices.

Not that it was idyllic, but in that era, a company's stakeholders consisted of devoted, lifetime employees, loyal customers, dependable suppliers, responsive distributors, and moderately involved boards of directors. That period of economic growth was also accompanied by a relatively favorable media, limited government regulation, less litigation, and few, if any, activist consumer groups. Of course there were labor and management concerns, as we have today, but the point is, the times were simpler and any surfacing issues could be isolated and quickly rectified.

From the 1950s through the early 1970s, long tenures for chief executives were common and dismissals were rare events. Many CEOs ran their businesses for ten to twenty years and their personas were inseparable from that of their company's identity. During those formative decades of modern commerce, retirement was usually the only way long-serving chief executives parted with their companies. And when CEOs were ready to retire—often at a time of their own choosing—they had a good idea as to whom their successor would be, as did most others in the organization, including the board.

The role of the incoming CEO was to maintain the business. The belief was that if the incoming CEO could stay the course, steadily gain market share, and control spending, the company would thrive for decades to come.

For most companies at the time, the requisite skill set of a succeeding CEO centered on understanding the company's products, markets, distribution channels, and competition. That candidate was most likely already on the executive team and in consideration for the top spot. In the 1950s, only one out of ten successors was hired from outside the company, and by the 1970s, only one out of seven.[1]

Boards of directors, at the time, were involved in overseeing major corporations, though their role in the CEO succession process was usually limited to being made aware of and approving the CEO's handpicked successor. If the CEO felt comfortable with the candidate, the board would take the CEO's lead. Board members would endorse the CEO's choice, but otherwise stayed on the sidelines and out of the process. They became involved only if a crisis—such as in the CEO's death—forced them to step in and name a successor.

Craig Sturken, chairman of the board of directors for Spartan Foods, Inc., remembers that business period as one of far less board involvement in CEO succession planning:

> It was easy to be aligned with the CEO and the company's business strategy. There were no external constituencies as we have today, tracking and blogging our every move. The trajectory of

the company was known to everyone in the organization and all of us on the board. We could see five to ten years out with a high degree of certainty and we easily approved the person the CEO recommended as his successor.

In those early years, there was little movement of employees from one company to another. As a result, employers knew a great deal about the personalities, talents, and skills of each executive. In the 1950s and 60s, *Fortune* 500 executives remained with their companies for an average of 24 years.[2] This stability epitomized the generational attitude at the time. The Silent Generation (1925–1942), born during the Great Depression and World War II made up over 90 percent of the workforce—vastly different when compared to the four generations at work today. They were labeled "silent" because of their withdrawn, cautious, and unadventurous orientation—understandable, given the hardships they encountered during their childhood years. They viewed work as an obligation and their sense of loyalty to their employer precluded them from leaving their companies for a better paying position elsewhere.[3]

Companies back then were not as interested in a potential successor's performance as they were in that person's character. Given the direct, linear path of business at the time, companies were content with sustaining success and advancing through incremental gains in the marketplace. As a result, employers spent more time shaping select executives to be market planners rather than market insurgents.

Dr. Alice Tybout, Harold T. Martin Professor of Marketing at the Kellogg School of Management at Northwestern University, notes:

> 'Checkers' is the perfect analogy for the way business was conducted in the United States and quite possibly was the mind frame of senior executives at most companies in developed and developing nations. Strategy involved linear moves that required a steady, trusted leader who knew the organization and its capabilities well. CEO succession planning was limited and boards accepted whomever the CEO chose as his successor. This approach worked reasonably well when the business climate was fairly predictable, as was the case through the 1970s. What many companies didn't realize, or prepare for, was just how much things could change in a few short years.

In the 1950s and 60s, there was a sense of confidence within the business community that almost any market problem could be solved and any challenge overcome. Companies such as GE, AT&T, Procter & Gamble, HP, and IBM became known as "academy" companies, patterning their development of leaders after the military model of bringing in new recruits, moving them through a series of jobs and training exercises, then advancing those who continue to perform well.

However, by the middle of the 1970s, CEOs and their boards began to realize that conducting business was becoming more difficult and less predictable. The economic upheavals of the 1970s—energy shortages, inflation, and the beginnings of international competition with companies such as Toyota, Nippon Steel, and Sony—revealed that corporate leadership had become somewhat inbred, habitual, and lethargic. Whether the result of being stuck in outdated traditions, fearful of risk and failure, or merely absorbed in denial, CEOs and their boards—across a number of industries—were slow to respond to the challenges they faced, and their companies' profits and share prices began to decline.

## Capture the King

By the 1980s and 90s, business had become more like a game of chess. Lateral moves were no longer enough to sustain a company's success. The game of simple battles had morphed into a game of campaigns with marketplace skirmishes occurring simultaneously and on different fronts.

Many companies were, for the first time, playing on a global stage, entering new markets, appealing to unfamiliar cultures, and contending with deep-rooted, in-country competitors. CEOs and their executive teams required newer skills including broader vision, cultural awareness, strategic alignment of resources, and thinking three or more moves in advance—a more challenging game, but still comprehensible.

Against this backdrop of dramatically changing market dynamics, compounded by more companies engaging in mergers and acquisitions as part of the business strategy du jour, the task of CEO succession became increasingly challenging, requiring greater deliberation, more attention to diverse talent retention and development, shorter tenures, and greater collaboration between the board and the CEO.

Proper CEO succession now necessitated an ongoing, well-administered process, a discipline few companies had to contend with prior to the 1980s. That requisite level of process and planning pushed against the demands of time and resources for many organizations. That reality, coupled with the need for growth in foreign markets, forced many CEOs, more than ever before—and in many instances for the first time in their company's history—to search outside the organization for their successor.

By searching externally for candidates, CEOs were conceding that their companies had a failed internal succession planning process and had not devoted enough time to talent development.

According to Michael Useem, director of Wharton's Center for Leadership and Change Management, "The trend line from 1970 to 2000 shows a slow but steady increase in the number of companies that look to the outside in the case of a departing CEO. At the start of that period, one in seven new CEOs at major companies came from outside the firm; by the end, one in four."[4]

As Tim O'Donovan, retired chair and CEO of Wolverine Worldwide Inc., sees it,

> From time to time, a company may face performance issues or the need for a significant shift in strategy. In those circumstances, it may be preferable and even necessary to look to an outside leader to be the catalyst for change and reinvigoration of the company.

The fast-changing business landscape of the 1980s and 90s forced many CEOs and their companies to shake off their denial and complacency in the face of change, attitudes that disabled American Express, Citibank, Digital, General Motors, IBM, Kodak, Tandy, Xerox, and so many others.

How quickly things changed. In 1980, Sears' marketing plans did not even mention Wal-Mart as a competitor, yet by the end of that decade, Wal-Mart had passed both Sears and Kmart to become America's largest retailer, and by 1992, employed more people than GM, Ford, and Chrysler combined. After Mercedes' sales in the United States dropped 24 percent in 1991, its top management finally conceded that it had to change its strategy because of Japanese competition. Until then, Mercedes' management refused even to acknowledge the existence of competition in its high-end market sector.[5]

Prior to the late 1970s, boards relied on the CEO to define and set the strategic direction of the company. Directors had little insight into the company's business and even less knowledge of the bench strength of the company's executive team. But in the 1980s and 90s, loss of market share and product failures caused such attitudes to change. Shareholders' increasing expectations for performance had a dramatic effect on the relationship between the board and the CEO, further deepening the involvement of the board in the strategic direction of the company.

A climate developed in which individual directors began to raise questions and debate the issues introduced by the CEO rather than merely approving their formal presentations. Boards began to take a more active role in understanding and responding to the CEO's strategic decisions, and took it upon themselves to become more fully informed in their company's businesses.

James P. Hackett, CEO and president of Steelcase, Inc. recalls it:

> Our more active participation in providing strategic oversight helped generate a better understanding of the strategic direction of the company as we approached the new millennium. It gave us a better understanding of the capabilities required of the company's leadership and the mindset and skills required of the CEO. We began to realize, I think for the first time, whether the CEO had the required talents needed to sustain the success of the organization.

## Decline in Confidence at the Top

At this time, and for the first time in any significant numbers, more and more chief executives began leaving their companies for a number of reasons other than retirement. Some CEOs were drawn away by competing firms offering more attractive opportunities. Many were taking their stock options and cashing out. Others were pushed out, well before retirement age, due to active takeovers or dismissals by their boards for poor company performance.

In addition to capturing the attention of boards, lackluster sales and profits also attracted the attention of Wall Street analysts to the issue of CEO selection. This magnified in the early 1990s when the boards of American Express, GM, IBM, Kodak, and Westinghouse fired their CEOs following prolonged periods of poor performance in the face of a rapidly changing business environment.[6]

The relatively sudden replacement of the CEOs with outsiders in these high-visibility companies—for the first time in their corporate histories—signified that qualified, internal successors were not being developed to assume the reins of responsibility.

In addition to losing their CEOs and any semblance of continuity in leadership, these multi-billion dollar international companies immediately lost investor confidence and stock price value. Statistics have shown that in planned CEO turnovers, a company's stock price will historically lose an average 0.8 percent value—a relatively stable retaining of market value. But in unplanned CEO turnovers, stock prices will lose an average 12.6 percent in value.[7]

While Wall Street may have commended the boards of these companies for taking the necessary step of replacing their CEOs, the reality was that these boards did not intervene until these huge companies reached a critical stage of failure, suggesting that the boards of each of these companies were not proactively engaged in leadership continuity planning. And, if board involvement in CEO succession planning was low or nonexistent at these *Fortune* 100 companies, what was not being practiced in the *Fortune* 1000?

At the close of the twentieth century, the sudden loss of confidence in these pillars of commerce increased the scrutiny of Wall Street analysts and heightened the expectations of shareholders—both seeking better corporate governance and improved stock performance. It also provoked government and consumer groups to take a closer look at and more active stance in regulating and influencing management activities in corporations.

In the decades of checkers and chess, the CEO led the succession process, making all major decisions regarding their successor and the timing of their transition. The board rarely acted to override the CEO's decisions or step into what was perceived as the CEO's turf.

However, by the end of the 1990s, the increasing complexity of business and high-profile failures in leadership continuity in a number of major corporations indicated that it was no longer wise to leave succession planning solely in the hands of the CEO. The growing expectation on the part of stakeholders was that CEO succession planning needed to be a continuous process and a shared responsibility between the CEO and the board—with the board having ultimate accountability for its thorough implementation and successful outcome.

## 3-D Chess: More Levels of Play—Less Certainty of Outcome

Today, the world of business is moving at a much greater pace than at any other time in history. In this constantly changing business climate, CEOs and their leadership teams make few decisions and take few actions with any degree of confidence or assurance of a successful outcome.

There is no longer a definitive endgame in sight for a CEO's actions in the marketplace—at least not within the time frame of the top leader's shortening tenure. The outcome of decisions made may not be known until several years later and most likely during the next CEO's administration. The game has morphed into one of three-dimensional chess where one move on one level can affect strategies and outcomes on a number of other fronts. Given this increased level of complexity, the reality of business in the twenty-first century is one of constant competitive uncertainty and unforeseen consequences—further complicated by more stakeholders demanding greater transparency and increased regulation.

Since 2000, the globalization of business and the interdependence of global economies have accelerated at an unprecedented rate. The speed of technological change, the internationalization of capital markets, the acceleration of regulatory requirements, and the diversity of the workforce and its changing generational attitudes have each impacted companies and their leaders. And to ratchet up an already frenetic condition, the severe global economic downturn in these most recent years has aggravated matters even more.

The business practices and market decisions of corporations and even the personal lives of their CEOs have become far more transparent than ever before. Executives operate under the constant surveillance of 24-hour news cycles. And just as the Internet has enabled even the smallest business to appear as large as a multinational corporation, an individual with a blog and a personal agenda against a company or CEO has the equivalence in reach and credibility as any international news outlet.

Internal stakeholders including employees, boards of directors, customers, suppliers, and increasingly more external constituents including government agencies, environmentalists, consumer groups, and other organizations have escalated their expectations for personal involvement. These stakeholders have moved from merely wanting to be informed to expecting to participate in and affect the decisions of the company.

CEO Doyle Beneby of CPS Energy describes the business climate today as one of increasing uncertainty:

> Throughout my career, I always felt I could solve problems with a reasonable chance of success. Yet, in today's business environment, I sense that events impinging on my company could really be—for the first time—out of my control. Moreover, I have to be very careful about statements made to the media for fear of being misconstrued. Every decision is scrutinized and can have an immediate effect on my company's stock price.

The recession that began in 2008 resulted in a number of unplanned CEO departures and outright dismissals, made very public by the media due to the severity of the current cycle of economic decline. Some companies were prepared to manage the sudden transitioning of their leadership, but as was discovered in the high-profile failures in the 1990s, many had no leadership continuity planning process in place. It seems not much has changed.

In 2008, eighty of the *Fortune* 100 appointed a new CEO with 45 percent of those companies going outside to find their successor.[8] While each of these companies had a CEO succession planning process in place, the fact that almost half of them had no internal successor ready to assume the top leadership position suggests that some of these companies may not be adequately preparing their internal candidates. Given that these are of the largest companies in the world with the depth of resources and drawing power for talent at all levels, something seems amiss.

Shareholders have become acutely aware of the need for CEO succession planning and change in a company's management is now one of the most important areas for investors to follow. Shareholders are also beginning to realize—especially given the high-profile departures and dismissals of CEOs—a greater need for corporate governance and that CEO succession planning depends, in large part, on a sound process originating at the board level.

In October 2009, the Securities and Exchange Commission issued guidance stating that "Companies should no longer expect to be allowed to evade shareholder proposals regarding CEO succession planning."[9] Reversing a long-held earlier position, the SEC now regards CEO succession planning as a "significant issue involving the governance of the corporation, that poor CEO succession planning poses too great a business risk, and that there should be greater transparency and shareholder disclosure about the management of succession." This change indicates that the SEC regulators have repositioned CEO succession as a "risk management issue" and places its responsibility in the boardroom and not in the office of the CEO.[10]

The tipping point for the SEC reversal may well have been the announcement by Ken Lewis, CEO of Bank of America Corporation, on September 30, 2009, that he would retire at the end of the year. It soon became apparent that Bank of America's board had no successor in place and would most likely have to bring someone in from the outside. The timing could not have been worse as this announcement came in the middle of the deepest recession in decades. Not only shareholders, but also the media and the public-at-large became keenly aware that the biggest bank holding company in the United States and one of the world's largest financial institutions had no successor to replace its departing CEO.

One of the earliest and most visible tests of the new SEC guidance came in February, 2011, on the heels of Apple CEO Steve Jobs' January announcement of an indefinite medical leave from the company. Central Laborers Pension Fund, a union in Jacksonville, Illinois introduced a proposal that called for Apple's board to spell out its criteria for choosing the next CEO. The union demanded that Apple name internal candidates for the job and that Apple begin a "non-emergency CEO succession planning" process and report on it to shareholders each year.

That same February, at Apple's annual shareholders' meeting, Apple's board urged its shareholders to vote against the union's proposal on the grounds that disclosing Apple's succession plans would give the company's competitors an unfair advantage. The board felt that such disclosure would encourage rivals to undermine Apple by luring away the company's high-value executives who were not in the running for the CEO position. The board also argued that revealing the company's succession plans could even affect Apple's ability to recruit new talent, whether they were executives or even engineers. The proposal was soundly rejected by shareholders and did not even pass the preliminary tally.

While it remains to be seen if any similar proposals by shareholder groups will succeed, it seems inevitable that boards will need to be more deeply involved in the way CEO succession planning is managed, and that from a selection of well-qualified candidates, a successor is ready to assume the top job.

Though we clearly agree with the SEC that CEO succession planning is a significant issue involving the governance of the corporation and that its absence poses too great a business risk, we consider it somewhat naïve to suggest that there be greater transparency about whom the candidates are and precisely how the process is being managed. Such guidance defies an understanding of business and any comprehension of the negative impact of such disclosures on a company—from the loss of talent internally to the competitive pressures externally.

Shareholders are right to expect that companies have a CEO succession process in place. There are far too many instances over the past 20 years of poor board governance and high-profile companies failing at leadership continuity. Because of highly visible failures in succession, demands for transparency from regulatory and activist groups have swung like a pendulum, overcompensating to an extreme. The only way to forestall such extreme demands is by boards being more proactively engaged, having a best-in-class CEO succession process in place, and persuasively communicating to their constituents their confidence in and accountability for that process.

## Far More Than the Transitioning of the Top Leader

It seems that the importance of the issue of CEO succession in this rapidly evolving business environment and the orientation and preparedness of board members are certainly at odds. This disconnect can be attributed to several factors: it is a challenging process, it takes time, and it may not be perceived as an urgent matter when compared to more immediate business issues. Moreover, the mere mention of succession planning conjures up a host of organizational dynamics and powerful psychological stress points, for issues of power, ego, legacy, and personal agendas have as much if not more influence on the process as objective data, procedures, and timelines. These factors and forces can cause complacency, hesitation, and reluctance on the part of board members. However, in the end, there are no reasons that justify ignoring the task. In short, it's difficult and can be messy work—but it is critical and must be managed.

Walt D'Alessio, who currently serves on such boards as Exelon Corporation (lead director), Independence Blue Cross (chairman), Brandywine Realty Trust (chairman) and Pennsylvania Real Estate Investment Trust (lead director), sees board involvement in CEO selection not as something board members should approach kicking and screaming, but an involvement driven by their own convictions.

I don't recall a time when board alignment with the company was more important than today. We need to have more communication and review of business strategy. We need to do a better job in selecting and grooming successors. The difficulty lies in all the other priorities facing boards and companies today. The other reason is a dynamic I see on every board I sit on—directors are fearful of stamping an expiration date on the forehead of the incumbent CEO and creating unnecessary horse races among executive team members.

The business environment has undergone a huge transformation over the past several decades—from the simplicity of commerce in the mid-twentieth century, to the market expansions and consolidations of the 1980s and 1990s, to the global interconnectedness of the current era. Because the intricacies involved in selecting a CEO have increased with each passing decade, the mindset of the past and the methods previously used will no longer guarantee success in today's business climate.

Our global age requires a new kind of leadership, an alignment of the board and the CEO on all business issues, and the continuous development of talent to ensure continuity of leadership and sustained business success. If properly attended to and thoughtfully executed, CEO succession can offer a company far more than the transitioning of its top leader. CEO succession can enable companies to envision new opportunities for growth, to realign and strengthen processes and systems throughout the enterprise, and enliven and unite employees with new hope and greater confidence.

As we will discover in Chapter 2, many companies have strengthened their CEO succession plans and processes to keep pace with the changing business landscape. They have made succession a business priority and found ways to contend with the undercurrent of powerful psychological forces embedded in the process. These companies have succeeded in transitioning their top leaders and have grown their enterprises as a result.

There are equally as many companies that have failed at succession. For many, the results are immediate, with the loss of stock value and the exodus of key talent. For others, the negative impact on their market position, operations, and ability to retain crucial talent will unfold in the years to come. There is hardly a more crucial process for an organization's continued health than CEO succession.

*"I think Alan Mulally will be a great mentor to a lot of our younger leaders. He's a great team builder. Our team needs the steady hand of someone who has been through a turnaround, someone who knows what it takes."*

—William Clay Ford, Jr., executive
chairman of the Ford Motor
Company

*"Not addressing CEO succession planning, whether because we felt it was lower priority or we just didn't want to deal with the personality issues, probably set our company back five years."*

—Board member of a *Fortune* 100
company (anonymity requested)

## A REOCCURRING PATTERN

A great deal of attention has centered on corporate governance in recent years, more so than at any other time in history. A direct line can be drawn from the corporate and accounting scandals at the onset of the twenty-first century, which cost investors billions of dollars when the share values of affected companies fell, to the

Sarbanes-Oxley Act of 2002. Most recently, the collapse of the financial markets in 2007, and realization that one of the world's largest financial institutions had no successor to step in at the unplanned departure of its CEO, coincided with the Securities and Exchange Commission revising its position on boards disclosing CEO succession plans to its shareholders.[1]

Today, stories that flood the networks and cable news channels with accounts of corporate failures are typically followed by the very public resignations or dismissals of the faltering companies' top leaders. In virtually every instance, corporate failure is directly attributed to a sitting CEO—the most visible, most responsible, and highest-salaried position in the company.

One reason for the heightened level of media attention is timing, as corporate failures tend to follow periods of economic growth—in other words, when economic decline sets in. As in a perfect inverse relationship, a descending economy raises media interest and the quest for answers. Questionable business practices are exposed, and economic turmoil attributed, in part, to corporate mistakes or misconduct. And to put faces on it, blame is placed at the feet of the fallen companies' top leaders, whose leadership may have been unassailable, but who are held responsible for the loss in shareholder value or public trust because it happened on their watch.

The most recent examples of the alternating cycles of success and failure are the high-profile financial scandals at the close of the twentieth century—most notably Enron, Tyco, and WorldCom—that followed the economic boom of the 1990s, and the 2008 collapse of financial institutions and crisis in the automotive industry that followed the recovery from the 2001 recession.

The pattern tends to repeat itself: Every business downturn and increase in press coverage leads to heightened stakeholder activism, especially among shareholders who, displeased with corporate performance, demand a change in leadership, greater board governance, and in some instances, greater government regulation.

Concurrent with the increased focus on corporate governance is the sheer volume of CEO turnover since the 1990s. A CEO's tenure, on a global average, is now 7.6 years, down from 9.5 years in 1995, and in the past two decades, 30 percent of *Fortune* 500 CEOs have lasted fewer than three years in office.[2] Other studies indicate that

40 percent of CEOs were dismissed or forced to resign within their first 18 months on the job.[3]

Since 2000, a number of studies have been conducted on CEO succession planning in the *Fortune* 500, with one annual study following CEO turnover among the world's top 2,500 public companies, categorizing and tracking succession events along three fronts:[4]

- Merger-driven, in which the CEO's job was eliminated once the two companies combined;
- Performance related, where the CEO was asked to leave or forced to resign by the board of directors; and
- Regular transition, in which the CEO retired, accepted a better position or opportunity elsewhere, or stepped down for health-related issues.

While regular transitions have accounted for approximately 50 percent of all CEO successions over the past 20 years, changeovers have become increasingly unplanned and, in some instances (and not for reasons related to the CEO's health), sudden. Moreover, the number of CEO turnovers arising from performance-related issues has steadily increased since 2000.

## Focusing on the Symptoms

Why do so many CEOs fail these days—especially within the first two years of office—compared to one or two generations ago? A number of books and articles have been written on the subject, many since 2000, attempting to pinpoint the reason or reasons for failure in leadership. These works suggest that chief executive failure is attributable to one of three problems: poor judgment, a lack of execution, or personality flaws such as ego, arrogance, or a command-and-control style of leadership that fails to engender employee trust and inspiration. In very few instances are the reasons for a CEO's failure attributed to a lack of experience, knowledge, or competence.

When you consider all the performance issues or character weaknesses associated with failed leadership, which of these imperfections are any different than those found in CEOs 20, 30, or even 50 years ago? Human nature is quite constant, but what has evolved over the decades is the pace and complexity of business. The result is greater failure now than at any other time in the past, even given the presence of the same flawed traits across that span of time.

Warren Buffett once said, "Only when the tide goes out do you discover who's been swimming naked."[5] The shortcomings in performance and character that have historically plagued leaders to one degree or another may not have been as apparent or consequential in the past as they are now. Therefore, attributing CEO failure to these deficiencies alone is, in a sense, placing too much blame on the symptoms and not enough on the underlying cause.

We are not suggesting that the increase in CEO turnover is solely the result of the relentless demands of a changing business environment—although the speed, complexity, and public scrutiny of business has certainly accelerated and accentuated the issue. Keep in mind that 40 percent of CEOs may be failing in their first 18 months of office, but 60 percent are not failing, are facing the challenges, and are succeeding.

## PINPOINTING THE CAUSE AND COST

The single most important issue underlying CEO failure and, consequentially, company failure, is an inadequate or poorly executed CEO succession plan that either put the wrong leader in the top position for the wrong reasons or did not attend to the necessary integration issues that should precede and follow the most important transitional event in a company's life.

Boards, when in the midst of a leadership crisis or an abrupt and unplanned departure, often focus on filling the position with a quickly vetted replacement. In some cases, boards, unfamiliar with or lacking confidence in the company's internal talent will bring in someone from the outside, thereby increasing the risk of CEO failure—regardless of how qualified that outside talent may be. In many of these instances, boards fail to devote enough attention to integrating an outside successor with the existing culture and strategic direction of the company. During the period 2000 to 2010, external hires resulted in almost twice the CEO failure rate when compared to inside successors.[6]

The most important and impactful decision any board of directors can make is the selection and de-selection of the CEO. Getting this decision right will undoubtedly have significant influence on the success of an organization, while getting it wrong can set in motion a series of disastrous events. Unfortunately, many boards do not fully embrace their share of the responsibility and ultimate accountability for the CEO succession process. Too often, they delegate that responsibility to the company's CEO, who has little time or, in some cases, desire for identifying his or her own successor.

The fallout from a CEO's unanticipated departure or sudden dismissal can prove very costly. There are the obvious direct costs including the CEO's compensation—with outside talent costing quite a bit more. Among the largest companies in 2007 and 2008, the median compensation for outside hires totaled $12.1 million, about *75 percent more* than the $6.9 million for internal hires. The gap in compensation was even greater for small companies where external recruits received a median of $3.6 million, more than twice the $1.6 million paid to internal successors.[7]

There are also the indirect costs that may not have an immediate impact on the business but may take their toll several years later, including errors in judgment, shortsighted strategies, poor or no execution, and missed marketplace opportunities. But, the costs that leave the deepest scars are the loss of stakeholder trust and confidence, the erosion of share value, and the exodus of future talent—at all levels of the organization.

To give credit where credit is due, many boards today are more aligned with the strategic direction of the companies they serve than ever before, are far more aware of the need for CEO succession planning than their predecessors, and are far more prepared with succession plans and processes in place. However, even with all this awareness and preparedness, most boards of directors are still beleaguered, to some degree, by the powerful psychological forces and organizational dynamics that prevent them from engaging in CEO succession planning. Board members' concerns include:

- Implying a lack of confidence in the CEO that may provoke an unplanned departure

- Showing a lack of allegiance to the CEO—the source of their personal wealth or position
- Spending valuable time on a non-critical path issue that may not occur for another three to five years
- Creating a "horse race" among internal candidates
- Causing an unnecessary exodus or disengagement of non-candidate executives

Effective CEO succession occurs when boards acknowledge that strong emotions are going to be a part of every leadership transition. For them, the duty of governance overrides personality issues or personal gains. Boards that are accepting of that reality step up to the challenge by putting in place processes that management and directors agree to and abide by at the onset, processes that—by their very presence and practice—help defuse emotional tension. Ineffective CEO succession occurs when boards deny and avoid the difficult challenges and concerns associated with succession planning. The result is an unpreparedness that exposes their companies to gaps and failures in leadership and costly errors in judgment.

Here are a few examples of companies in recent years that have done very well in weathering the changing business landscape while maintaining exceptional performance. Unfortunately, there are just as many examples of companies that have suffered breaks in performance, missed windows of opportunity, or descending market value and competitiveness.

What separates the successful from the unsuccessful—the root cause—is a board of directors, duty bound, accountable, and prepared for the planned or unplanned transitioning of the CEO.

## THE BENEFITS OF SUCCESS

### MasterCard

MasterCard Inc. performed quite well with Robert Selander as its CEO. Under Selander's leadership from 1997 to 2010, MasterCard transformed from a 40-year-old membership association into one of the world's leading companies, responsible for shaping today's electronic payments industry. In 2009, *Barron's* cited Selander's leadership as a critical reason behind its decision to rank MasterCard first in the *Barron's* 500.[8]

When Selander was ready to retire, the board, which he chaired, vetted and recruited Ajay Banga from Citigroup as president in order to orient and integrate Banga into the company a full year prior to making him CEO in July 2010.

Now, after one year in office, the company has moved to an even higher level of performance under Banga's leadership. With a renewed business strategy compellingly communicated by Banga to Wall Street analysts and investors, the stock price has soared more than 50 percent with the company's market capitalization increasing by more than $15 billion—even in the face of regulatory pressures that will impact MasterCard's revenues.

While it's still early in Ajay Banga's tenure, it appears MasterCard will maintain its strong success trajectory. The company's ability to advance its solid business footing is attributable to how well the board of directors managed the succession process. This included the board's involvement and alignment with the strategic direction of the company, identifying Banga as the ideal candidate with the necessary global experience and cultural perspectives, and assimilating Banga for a full year with Selander as his tutor, ensuring a successful integration process.

## McCormick

In January 2008, Robert Lawless, chairman, president, and CEO of McCormick & Company, Inc., stepped down after 11 years as chief executive officer of the Baltimore-based spice company to make way for Alan Wilson, an internal candidate who had been mentored by Lawless and groomed for five years prior to becoming CEO.

Under Lawless' leadership, McCormick had grown steadily from $1.7 billion in 1996 to nearly $3 billion in 2007, and the company's market cap had more than doubled over that same period. Since Alan Wilson took office in 2008, the company has accelerated its ten-year growth rate of 5 percent to 8 percent with double-digit increases in both sales and profit for the second quarter of fiscal year 2011. McCormick's global footprint expanded substantially during Lawless' term; it has grown even larger under Alan Wilson with Lawless as an open and willing advisor. At the onset of 2011, McCormick announced that it would acquire a leading flavor brand in Poland, a majority interest in a joint venture in India, and work towards new product innovation and expanded distribution in China. The company expects more than 12 percent of 2012 sales to come from emerging markets, up from 9 percent in 2010.[9]

McCormick's board of directors determined early on that a well-executed CEO succession plan would enable the company to sustain its solid business footing and maintain its people-oriented culture by developing talent from within.

McCormick's board also came to the realization years ago that it is much easier to advance a succession plan agenda when business is running smoothly than under the stress of difficult and uncertain times. By making succession planning an ongoing process, McCormick intends never to be in a position where the board will compromise its judgment with an untested internal candidate or feel pressured to hire an outsider, creating a cultural or strategic mismatch. As Lawless puts it, "Organizational leaders have many opportunities and challenges in today's business environment, but one of the most important is the legacy of leadership."[10]

## IBM

In 1993, IBM's board of directors fired John Akers and was forced to go outside for his successor. The boards of several high-visibility companies at the time, including American Express, GM, Kodak, and Westinghouse, also fired their CEOs for declining business performance and brought in outside successors—the first time in each of these companies' histories. Each had failed to develop a CEO successor and IBM was no different. The changing business environment that suddenly accelerated in the 1990s caught many companies unprepared, ungoverned, and embarrassingly leaderless.

During Akers' tenure from 1985 to 1993, the world was moving to desktop computing while IBM remained fully invested in mainframes with a CEO paralyzed by indecisiveness, and a complacent, strategically disengaged board who, in 1991, publicly expressed its full confidence in Akers.[11]

At the time Akers left office, the company had posted a $5 billion annual loss, the largest single loss in corporate history. The dividend dropped from $1.21 to 54 cents, after the company failed to make enough profit to cover its dividend payments for two consecutive years.

Although IBM was the largest computing company in the world when Louis Gerstner took over in 1993, it was on the verge of collapse under the weight of its own debt—a situation Gerstner reversed in two years through fiscal responsibility and a number of other changes. Gerstner cut long-term debt from $14.6 to $9.9 billion and boosted IBM's share price from less than $140 to $168. By 1995, IBM had stabilized and by 1999 Gerstner was leading one of the most respected companies in corporate America.

IBM had its epiphany. Succession planning at IBM today is a best-in-class model of leadership continuity—at all managerial levels and on every continent. That excellence was demonstrated again in the succession from Gerstner to Sam Palmisano and most recently, in the handoff of the CEO role to Ginny Rometty. It is a comprehensive, staged process owned by a fully engaged and strategically aligned board of directors. A core responsibility of the CEO is to identify and test the mettle of three to four successors—a selection not based on skill as much as it is based on the way in which each high potential responds to challenges as they move through various assignments within the organization.

## Johnson & Johnson

With more than 250 companies and operating in 60 countries, Johnson & Johnson has maintained an incredible level of positive stability, grown steadily, and led on many market fronts for close to 40 years. It has remained one of the top five most respected companies in the world, along with having one of the most respected boards of directors.[12]

Ralph Larsen, J&J's CEO from 1989 to 2002, gave hundreds of speeches around the enterprise to encourage employees from all the companies under the corporate banner to unite and focus on the same goals. J&J's sales grew from $10 billion to $33 billion during Larsen's 13-year tenure, and its market cap soared from $16 billion in 1989 to $192 billion by the time he stepped down in April 2002. Larsen dealt with his corporate challenges just as his predecessor, James Burke, did during his tenure from 1976 to 1989 amidst the Tylenol crisis.

Since the end of 2002, the stock has returned about 3.5 percent annually, slightly better than the S&P 500 healthcare index because of J&J's high dividend yield. J&J's annual revenue has jumped by about 70 percent since 2002, with sales per employee growing at a faster rate than its rivals, Procter & Gamble, Pfizer, and Medtronic.[13]

The company attributes a major part of its continuous growth to the effective implementation of its ongoing succession planning programs. For almost two generations, Johnson & Johnson's management and educational training as well as specialized individual development programs have provided the company with managers and leaders ready to step in and fill key positions all over the world. Candidates are found in many of the companies under the J&J corporate banner—individual profit-and-loss centers that provide perfect testing grounds for future leadership talent.[14]

As a demonstration of Johnson & Johnson's succession planning competence, half of the company's CEOs, throughout its 125 years of operations, has risen from within the organization.

## McDonald's

Succession planning at McDonald's Corporation is an often-told story, though worth revisiting, as it is probably the best contemporary illustration of how succession planning can help a company maintain business continuity, even in the sudden and unexpected transitioning of a leader, and in McDonald's case, the sudden transitioning of two leaders, back-to-back.

When CEO Jim Cantalupo unexpectedly died in April 2004, the board was able to appoint a successor, Charles Bell, in an orderly manner, just six hours later. Only a few weeks into his new tenure, Bell was diagnosed with cancer. He stepped down six months later and died in 2005. Again, there was a planned successor in the pipeline. The board was able to execute a quick and orderly succession with Jim Skinner.

Even though the board took only hours to name Bell's successor, McDonald's had been grooming Skinner for years. Having worked with Cantalupo and Bell on devising the marketing, product development, and restaurant improvement plans for McDonald's, Skinner was prepared to assume the role of CEO, not just to maintain the status quo, but to continue to grow the business.

Though there were two sudden, consecutive CEO deaths, between 2004 and 2007, McDonald's revenues grew 27 percent to $22.8 billion in that same period, and the company posted 9 percent growth in operating income to $3.9 billion.

The succession pipeline that produced Cantalupo, Bell, and Skinner began with a mandate from the board in 1998, to create a succession plan that would identify two successors for each key position in the company—"one ready now, one ready future." The "ready now" candidate had to be as least as strong as the person to be replaced, and the "future" candidate ready within two years.[15]

## THE COST OF FAILURE

## HP

The board of directors of HP announced on September 30, 2010, the election of Leo Apotheker as chief executive officer, making Apotheker, the former CEO of SAP, the third consecutive outsider recruited as CEO in HP's corporate history.

Carly Fiorina, the first outside successor, served between 1999 and 2005. She resigned in 2005 in a dispute with the board over the company's future. HP's stock lost half its value under Fiorina's tenure, though it is true that many tech companies struggled when the tech stock market bubble burst at the time she was hired. A core element in Fiorina's dispute with the board was the HP-Compaq merger in 2002, which was widely regarded as a strategic failure.[16]

Mark Hurd, the second outside recruit, succeeded Fiorina's in 2005. During Hurd's five-year tenure, he was able to boost earnings per share, his own pay (he was number four on CNNMoney's top 20 highest paid CEOs in 2009), and the company's stock price through acquisitions, cost cuts, and stock buybacks, but created little organic growth. In August 2010, the board voted for Hurd's resignation after an investigation into his involvement in a sexual harassment complaint and his alleged falsification of approximately $20,000 in expense reports to conceal that relationship.

Though HP's stock price closed up at $46.35 the day before the announcement of Hurd's resignation, it never, throughout his five years in office, rose to the levels last seen in 2000, during the first year of Carly Fiorina's term. HP's stock price instantly dropped 12 percent on the news of Hurd's leaving and continued to drop with growing realization of a leadership void as the largest company in one of the world's fastest moving industries operated for two months without a leader.[17]

HP's board had no formal succession plan in place when it hired Fiorina, Hurd, or Apotheker, who was rushed into the position two months after Hurd's forced resignation. HP's dismal market performance between 2000 and 2010—a decade of remarkable advances in technological innovation and marketplace gains by many incumbent and emerging high-tech firms, may seem the result of CEO failure, but the underlying cause can be directly attributed to the lack of board governance and succession planning and preparedness.

A lack of leadership continuity invariably leads to a loss of business continuity. The outcome for HP has been a decade of declining stock value and diminished earnings, missed market opportunities, and the exodus of high-tech talent.

## Bank of America

In 2001, Bank of America's CEO and chairman Hugh McColl stepped down and named Ken Lewis his successor. McColl was the architect in the creation of Bank of America, accomplished through a series of acquisitions throughout his tenure. During the company's formation, McColl handpicked each of the board members as well as his successor, Ken Lewis.

Lewis, following in the footsteps of McColl, started his tenure as CEO with what he called a "blank sheet of paper," listing all the companies he wanted to acquire in Bank of America's drive to be dominant in every financial product.[18]

The acquisition binge that began with McColl in the late 1990s culminated in the acquisitions of Merrill Lynch and Countrywide Financial in 2008. Lewis had grown the enterprise impressively, but with the economic swoon beginning in the fall of 2007, Bank of America's value plummeted. Forced to take a $45-billion bailout through the Tarnished Asset Relief Program, together with relentless public and regulatory scrutiny, Lewis blind-sided the board and investors in October 2009 by announcing his resignation in December of that same year.

When the stock market peaked in October 2007, Bank of America led all financial services companies in the S&P 500 with a market value of $124.2 billion and share price of $52.50. By the end of the first quarter of 2009, the company's market value had fallen to $19.7 billion with a share price of $3.17—about the same share price in 1984 when the company was known as BankAmerica.[19]

The rise and fall of Bank of America is not so much a story of CEO failure as it is one of poor board stewardship. Unlike the level of foresight and preparedness of McDonald's board, the board of directors of the largest bank holding company in the United States with over $3 trillion in assets had no successor in place when Ken Lewis announced his resignation. It's unthinkable— no, unacceptable—that a company of this size and significance should be so ill-prepared. Bank of America's board made several unsuccessful overtures to outside executives in search of a replacement for Lewis. Rebuffed in the effort to find a qualified successor from outside the company, the board and company's reputation suffered considerable embarrassment, and the ripple effect of this company's failure was felt by tens of millions of individuals the world over.

## Newell Rubbermaid

Newell Manufacturing acquired Rubbermaid in 1999, and the boards of this troubled merger became one, with the two halves not agreeing on corporate direction (cost containment versus marketing and sales). Without an understanding of the real threat to the business, no strong corporate structure over the held companies, and no succession plan in place, the board made an impulsive, emergency decision at the resignation of CEO John McDonough and hired Joseph Galli, Jr., as his successor.

Galli was a mercurial leader, skilled in sales and marketing—but not in manufacturing. During his tenure, Galli closed more than 80 facilities—including the historic company headquarters for both Newell and Rubbermaid. In doing so, Galli eliminated more than 5,000 jobs and increased the percentage of labor conducted in low-cost countries from 5 percent to 50 percent. Newell Rubbermaid struggled during Galli's term, posting a loss of more than $160 million in profits in 2003 and 2004 combined. In 2004, sales fell 2 percent to less than $4.9 billion and in the first half of 2005, dropped an additional 4 percentage points to $3 billion. Galli was eventually forced out in 2005.[20]

Mark Ketchum, a P&G veteran and board member, accepted the interim CEO position in 2005. In January 2011, Ketchum stepped down and in July 2011, Michael Polk, a board member and executive of Unilever, was hired as Ketchum's successor. The ten-year-standing problem of no succession plan, shareholder concerns about who was going to lead Newell Rubbermaid, and what the strategic direction of the company would be has negatively affected the company's stock price since the merger itself in 1999.

Johnson & Johnson's conglomerate of decentralized companies—similar in structure to that of Newell Rubbermaid—has proven a perfect breeding ground for future talent, with managers having the opportunity to run their own businesses and prove themselves capable of the broader assignment of CEO. But without board alignment on the strategic direction of the company and lacking a succession process that identifies and develops internal talent, Newell Rubbermaid has yet to use its held companies in a similar fashion as a test track for internal talent.

## Boeing

Phil Condit, who joined Boeing in 1965 and succeeded Frank Shrontz in 1996 as CEO and chairman of the board, abruptly resigned in December 2003—a sudden resignation that may have been caused by the defense contracting scandals that ultimately sent two Boeing executives to jail. His seven-year term was punctuated by "flawed strategy, questionable acquisitions, manufacturing controversies, and the ethical lapses at the company that jeopardized important contracts with the government."[21]

If Boeing's board could overlook Condit's strategic and operational mistakes, it could no longer tolerate the mounting ethics scandals with its biggest customer—the U.S. government. Sixty-eight-year-old Harry Stonecipher, former CEO of McDonnell Douglas, was brought back from retirement to succeed Condit in 2003, and 15 months later, resigned because of an improper relationship with a Boeing executive. The board immediately recruited board member Jim McNerney, CEO of 3M, to step in as Boeing's CEO in 2005.

During the CEO scandals of 2003 and 2004, Airbus overtook Boeing in the commercial jet market, forcing Boeing to lay off 40,000 employees in its commercial airplane division. In addition, the company lost $1 billion in military contracts due to a ban imposed by the Air Force on Boeing for illegally acquiring thousands of sensitive documents belonging to rival Lockheed Martin.[22] The ethical crisis also jeopardized Boeing's long-sought tanker deal, valued at more than $20 billion in 2003, but eventually awarded to Boeing in February 2011 for $35 billion.[23]

Beyond not having a CEO succession process in place in the world's largest aerospace company, Boeing's board was not attentive enough in vetting and challenging Condit's decisions, actions, and business dealings during his tenure.

Having to bring a CEO out of retirement only occurs in a vacuum of CEO succession planning. Considering the bench strength of a company the size of Boeing—from aviation engineers, to experienced defense personnel, to successful division heads—it would stand to reason that Boeing has the depth of talent worth retaining and developing. Take Alan Mulally.

In 2006, Alan Mulally, CEO of the Boeing Commercial Airplanes division, who widely praised as the major architect in Boeing's return as the world's dominant builder of commercial aircraft, left Boeing after 37 years to accept the CEO position at Ford Motor Company. In two years, Mulally transformed Ford into a profitable company once again, achieving $9.3 billion in profits in 2008 and 2009 combined.[24] In June 2011, Alan Mulally was named CEO of the Year by *Chief Executive* magazine.

## WHAT LIES BENEATH THE SURFACE

When we peer deeper into each of the examples of successful CEO succession, we see management and boards sharing responsibility for the CEO succession process and boards accepting full accountability for the continuous and effective execution of that entire process. We see boards recognizing that a succession process with definition, discipline, and the consent of management and directors, minimizes the difficult and sometimes disagreeable task of managing personalities and emotions. We see boards learning that continuous succession planning—especially during the best of times—means not having to make hasty decisions during the worst of times.

What lies beneath the surface of success—the root cause of success—are boards that have recognized the fact that CEO succession planning is far more than the transitioning of a company's leadership. When effectively and efficiently executed, CEO succession planning ensures the progression of a company's strategic direction, the continuity of its culture, and the retention and growth of its talent.

Conversely, in each example of failed leadership transition, we see boards lacking alignment on the strategic direction of the company, whether due to an unfamiliarity with or disagreement about the real business issues facing the company. As a result, and in virtually every instance, we see the selection and placement of the wrong talent for the wrong reasons. We also see boards unwilling or unable to confront personality-related issues either among themselves or with the CEO. Most of all, we see directors complacent or lacking a sense of urgency until an unplanned departure forces the board to look outside the company for a quick fix and hope for salvation.

What lies beneath the surface of failure—the root cause of breaks in a company's performance, missed windows of opportunity, or falling market value and competitiveness—are boards that have not yet recognized the fact that CEO succession planning is far more than the transitioning of a company's leadership.

Managing the CEO succession process is a board's greatest responsibility and a frequently managed and closely followed succession plan is essential in attending to that responsibility. Without fail, the costs of avoiding or sidestepping this process are far greater than the temporary challenges of managing a forceful personality or standing strong and as one during an emotionally charged moment.

Clearly, CEO succession planning is fundamental to the success or failure of a company. When done well, it enables a company to maintain its business heading, develop and retain its talent, and build on its market position—not just to stay the course—but to stand on the shoulders of its own success and attain even greater levels of performance with each transitioning leader.

# WHOSE JOB IS IT, ANYWAY?

## 3

*"The board has to understand, not just explicitly, but intuitively, that CEO succession planning is its most critical responsibility. If the board truly does understand that instinctively, then it will constantly be working the succession issue and it will always see the process in the context of a continuum."*

—John Hanson, non-executive
chairman and former CEO of
Joy Global, Inc.

Over the past 66 years, we have witnessed tremendous change permeate virtually every industry, with each passing decade bringing greater complexity to the course and conduct of business. Correspondingly, we have experienced the process of CEO selection and succession become far more involved and the repercussions of success or failure far more consequential.

The increase in CEO failures since the 1990s has repeatedly led to a loss of business continuity for many corporations. We have all seen companies squander their competitive edge and stall forward momentum due to a leadership vacuum. We've seen pinnacles of business, once thought too big to fail, lose billions in market value—precisely because of an inadequately conceived or carelessly executed

CEO succession plan that put the wrong leader in the top position, often without adequate support for the integration of that leader into the company's culture and leadership context.

The hands-off mindset and eleventh-hour methods of the past are no guarantees of success in the present, and, in many instances, cannot assure an organization of maintaining its status quo. Whether because of indifference, denial, or uncertainty, far too many boards have not embraced the reality that in this competitive environment, loss of leadership continuity *is* loss of business continuity.

Contrastingly, many boards, having experienced both successful and failed successions, concede that now—more than ever before—there is no room for failure. As a result, boards have been coming to grips with the issue of succession planning, striving to learn and adopt best practices to safeguard their company's future and remain a step ahead of the increasing demands and expectations of stakeholders.

## BEST PRACTICE VERSUS REAL PRACTICE

Over the past several years, RHR's clients' requests for assistance and support in CEO successions and transitions have increased tenfold. This has prompted us to create a special global practice with sharp focus on CEO succession, and broaden our understanding of the gap that exists today between best practice and real practice.

We began with an internal examination of the experience and collective insights of RHR's global force of management psychologists and consultants. This preliminary assessment of our own experiences and knowledge helped us formulate a comprehensive set of board member survey questions and an in-depth discussion guide for interviews with directors and CEOs pertaining to the succession planning process. We then proceeded with the following studies:

- RHR and Directorship, a board advisory company, conducted joint surveys of 386 board members with questions on governance including CEO/board relations, the impact of the Sarbanes-Oxley Act, CEO performance and compensation, CEO succession, and board dynamics.[1]
- In conjunction with *Chief Executive* magazine, RHR surveyed 236 directors exclusively on the topic of CEO succession to determine

how well their firms were positioned to deal with current and future succession events.[2]

- RHR conducted 41 in-depth interviews with directors (who collectively serve on more than 100 boards) about their experiences and lessons learned in both successful and unsuccessful CEO successions.[3]

## A Force Behind the Inertia

Without question, the directors we surveyed en masse and held in-depth discussions with are of the most experienced and ambitious individuals in the world of business, many of whom are current or former CEOs and top-tier executives of their own *Fortune* 500 companies. As board members, they assume the additional shared responsibility of acting as the highest governing authority of the companies they serve, protecting shareholder assets, selecting the CEO and appropriating compensation, recommending stock splits and share repurchasing programs, approving the company's financial statements, and supporting or dismissing acquisitions and mergers.

Yet, in our research, we uncovered a palpable ambivalence toward CEO succession planning, a reluctance-to-engage syndrome that has created a serious chasm between the *actual* practice of succession planning and what *best* practice ought to be.

The point is, directors are not passive toward CEO succession because of inexperience, a lack of business acumen, or waning self-confidence. Directors know what needs to be done and why; yet, in many instances, they never fully engage a comprehensive process! This is one of the most important findings in our research and in our practice. There are constraining forces that prevent a large percentage of directors from engaging in what is arguably their most important responsibility—transitioning the top leader.

Ninety-five percent of the 236 directors polled in our joint survey with *Chief Executive* magazine acknowledged that CEO succession is a business continuity issue—that the smooth transitioning of a company's top leader ensures the sustained success of an enterprise. (See Figure 3.1.) Yet, despite the seriousness of the responsibility and their role in the governance of the companies they serve, less than half of the directors surveyed rated themselves as capable in CEO succession planning.[4]

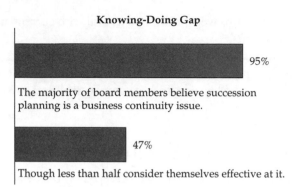

Figure 3.1: Knowing-Doing Gap

## INEFFECTIVE IN THEIR MOST CRITICAL ROLE

Fifty-three percent of the respondents to our survey assessed themselves as "ineffective" in executing their responsibilities in the CEO succession process. This is sadly consistent with other research findings over the past several years as board members have, year-on-year, rated CEO succession as one of their most crucial responsibilities, yet an area in which they are least effective.[5]

A pattern of responses on the cause of ineffectiveness emerged in both our surveys and in-depth interviews, all pointing to the absence of a well-developed and frequently administered CEO succession plan that is rigorous in nature with role clarity and definable accountabilities:

- 67% cite too few qualified candidates to select from;
- 60% feel their skills in interviewing are inadequate;
- 50% feel ineffective due to a strong director-candidate relationship;
- 44% claim there's not enough time; and,
- 41% admit that they give too much credence to the candidate's resume

Sixty-seven percent of directors claiming that there are "too few good candidates" suggest that boards simply are not managing CEO succession well enough in advance and that company management is not adequately identifying and preparing potential successors. This lack of internal talent development drives boards to look outside for successors, resulting in double the compensation for an externally hired CEO and double the failure rate.[6] Despite ten years of statistics confirming this likely outcome, active development of internal talent is still not the norm in many *Fortune* 500 companies. Half the board members surveyed said that their power over the succession process was compromised and ineffective when a director has a strong prior relationship with a candidate, thus creating a reluctance on the part of board members to question or challenge that relationship—even when the majority of the board members know that the "favored" candidate may not be the optimal choice as successor. This is consistent with our understanding of the personality issues and emotional tensions that accompany virtually every CEO succession event and a fundamental reason why so many intelligent, experienced, and well-intentioned directors shy away from the challenge.

On the issue of timing, only 30 percent of those surveyed believe that succession planning should be a continuous process while 34 percent consider six months to a year for a non-emergency CEO succession as an adequate planning horizon. One understands why 44 percent claim there's not enough time.

Only 8 percent of board members surveyed believe that succession planning should be more than two years in advance of a transition. In the corporate successes and failures cited in Chapter 2, each successful company cited (McCormick, Johnson & Johnson, McDonald's) views CEO succession as a continuous process and plans the transitioning of its leader two to five years in advance.

Another major area of ineffectiveness involves the evaluation skills of board members. Sixty percent admit that their interviewing skills are inadequate. Forty-one percent say they rely too much on the candidate's resume, while 40 percent believe there is a lack of candor in the interview process altogether. Candidates at this level have an enormous amount of experience in the interview process. Moreover, boards who are comparing an internal candidate with known imperfections to a polished outsider with a clean slate and an impressive resume can be misled or unduly influenced. And with the lack of preparation and resulting pressure to make snap selection decisions, impulsive choices of poorly vetted candidates are often made to the detriment of the company and its stakeholders.

## Awareness of the Risks

After reviewing the results of our research, one would conclude that board members may not be aware of the inherent liabilities associated with failed CEO transitions. This is not the case. When asked to inventory the risks, 83 percent of board members cited a loss of senior-level talent as the greatest downside, while 74 percent pointed to the loss of business momentum. Sixty-two percent of board members acknowledge that CEO turnover can have a negative impact on the company share value while 42 percent recognize that a failed CEO transition could result in the loss of customers. (See Figure 3.2.)

Board members are keenly aware of the risks associated with a failed CEO succession, but our experience, affirmed by our survey, suggests that there's a reluctance to own the process, whether due to feelings of inadequacy or ineffectiveness, or because they do not wish to become embroiled in the web of personality issues and emotional tensions that emerge at every step of the succession process.

The overwhelming majority of board members surveyed who indicate that CEO succession is a "business continuity issue" defines that loss in continuity as loss of senior-level talent, loss of business momentum, declining share value, and loss of customers. Why then would a board fail to take a good hard look at its own processes for addressing

Figure 3.2: Awareness of the Risks of a Failed CEO Transition

what is arguably its number one job—a responsibility that can determine, in one vote—the course and fate of the companies they serve?

## CHANGING TIMES, CHANGING MINDS

As we noted in Chapter 1, the business environment in the decades leading up to the close of the twentieth century was relatively simple and predictable compared to the pace and complexity of business today. Yet with all that has changed in the conduct of business, the discipline of CEO succession planning has not kept pace and advanced accordingly.

In our survey, we set out to determine the percentage of directors who accept the responsibility for the CEO succession process and how confident and prepared directors are in ensuring a smooth CEO transition process. We do see board members adjusting to the changing times and the increasing pressures from both internal and external stakeholders, but not to the degree that we expected.

When asked who has responsibility for the CEO succession process, inclusive of planning, selection, and integration, 48 percent of the 236 directors surveyed, cite that the responsibility resides specifically with the CEO. Fifty-seven percent claim that they did not know when their CEO plans to step down, suggesting that directors in our survey have not yet planned an end-of-term date with the CEO, or that the CEO has failed to disclosed his or her departure plans to the board. (See Figure 3.)

**An Important Job, But Whose Is It?**

Though 95% believe CEO succession is a business continuity issue:
48% of directors believe it's the CEO's responsibility.
57% don't know when their CEO plans to step down.
40% are not prepared for an emergency succession.

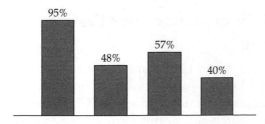

Figure 3.3: An Important Job, But Whose Is It?

An emergency succession plan ensures the continuous coverage of executive duties and safeguards the interests of the company's stakeholders, reputation, and value-creating activities. An emergency succession plan also provides guidelines to the board for temporarily appointing an interim CEO. Yet 40 percent of the directors surveyed claim that they are not prepared for an emergency succession in the event of a sudden, unexpected, or unplanned departure of their company's top leader.

Though 95 percent of the directors surveyed believe the company's stability and competitiveness is dependent upon continuity in leadership, the weight that board members place upon the importance of business continuity and their actual preparedness in succession planning are certainly at odds. Far too great a percentage considers itself ineffective, uninformed, and unprepared.

## Directors Share the Factors that Contribute to Success

In addition to conducting surveys with over 800 directors, we set out to conduct one-on-one in-depth interviews with 41 board members with the experience of having collectively served on the boards of 120 companies.

The purpose of these in-depth interviews was to discover what directors, in their own words, define as success in CEO succession and to provide examples of their experience with both successful and failed successions. Our intent was to learn of the conditions and cultures that create or prevent success in CEO succession planning. A number of themes emerged from the interviews, shedding some important light on this issue. Here are just a few of the comments of directors regarding the conditions for success in CEO succession:

## Insisting it be an Active, Not Passive, Undertaking

Douglas Conant, former CEO, and current director of Campbell Soup Company, believes success is dependent upon candid, transparent dialogue between the incumbent CEO and the board regarding tenure and retirement. In this fashion, there are no surprises, everyone on the board feels connected to the process, and the CEO and board can begin to orchestrate candidate development planning with good intentions and realistic timelines.

> I think it starts with the relationship that the CEO has with the board. I think it's absolutely essential that whoever is shepherding that relationship, whether it's a non-executive chairman or board member, ensures that there [is] good, transparent, candid dialogue between the CEO and the board regarding the CEO's intentions about his or her departure plans. And I think that discussion must allow [for] plenty of time in order to work through the process in a thoughtful way. So I advocate transparency, candor, and timeliness of dialogue as a primary foundation for success.
>
> The second thing I feel is essential is that ultimately someone on the board must own the process of moving things forward. You have to find the right person to work with the CEO and work with the board, but there must be an individual who advances the succession process in an inclusive way where everyone has a chance to be heard. It's critically important that the board be fully engaged in the process. This can't be a passive undertaking—it has to be active.
>
> The third element I have found helpful is involving a third party to help round out the thinking, and create a profile of success that encompasses internal planning but also brings best of class external thinking to the succession process.[7]

## Frequent and Candid Review of the Candidates

James Balloun, retired chairman and chief executive officer of Acuity Brands, Inc., believes that success in CEO succession comes from a frequent and candid review of all the candidates—a formalized process that is simple, transparent, and most importantly, in writing.

> All of these rankings that professional HR types like to use, in my view, are very destructive to the process. You know, where there are 48 characteristics of a leader, and the candidate is

ranked on each characteristic on a scale of one to five. The rankings are then added and divided by 48 in order to create a comparative score. That process creates a terrible vacuum in communication and in the honest and thoughtful assessment of a candidate.

My preferred approach is handled on one side of one sheet of paper. On the left-hand side is what I like about the candidate, on the right-hand side is what the candidate needs to improve, and on the bottom is my candid, overall assessment of the candidate's prospects. There is something wonderfully disciplining about putting that in front of candidates, having them read it, and then having a half-hour discussion about it. This tends to build trust between the board, the CEO, and the candidate because they are all looking at the same evaluation.[8]

## Working Through the Emotions

James Hackett, chief executive officer and president of Steelcase, Inc., also confronts the personal and emotional issues present in all CEO succession events, especially in the event the process creates a horse race among successor candidates.

CEO succession is a contact sport, so you don't want to think of it as a polite, ceremonial thing. You need to accept the fact that it will be an emotionally charged process with a great deal of intimacy, high involvement of all players, and difficult discussions. You've got to accept what this entails and work through the issues to where you're more focused on the benefits, not the difficulties, associated with a well-executed succession planning effort. That will carry you and convince you to go through with it.

The weaknesses and difficulties will be there so don't try to convince yourself that they'll go away. Accept the fact that they're going to be there. Realize that no succession is perfect because humans aren't perfect. Fully understand what you're getting into and why, accept the difficulties that lie ahead, then focus on the greater good.[9]

## Keeping Options Open Until the End

Ajay Banga, president and chief executive officer, MasterCard Worldwide, addresses head-on an issue that negatively affects 50 percent of the directors in our survey, forcing them to shy away from the personal and emotional dynamics that accompany most all successions.

> What corrupts the impartiality and thoughtfulness of the process is that once a search committee is formed and a board goes through the process of identifying each of the candidates, the board seldom goes through the diligence of objectively assessing all four or five candidates. What often destroys a good process is when one board member has come to the conclusion on which contender he or she wants and pushes and guides the process along to ensure that the preferred candidate wins. Aside from the loss of impartiality and potential selection of a less-than-optimum successor, this kind of favoritism leads to the certain loss of internal talent who regard the process as flawed, unfair, and unwinnable.[10]

## Letting the Process Provide the Answers

Mark Jennings, managing partner at Generation Partners, has served on the boards of 22 companies over the past 19 years and also believes success is in keeping candidate options open until the end of the process. For Jennings, it's a matter of not rushing to judgment simply in order for the board to appear organized and decisive to its stakeholders. A well-developed and openly administered process will allow the best candidate to emerge.

> Given the pressure of perception by stakeholders, it's most tempting to make a quick change and select the CEO successor so there appears to be smoothness and consensus among the board. The reality is that the cost is very high in presenting a false front. It's worth dealing with the short-term pain associated with openness and transparency in order to ensure a good long-term good fit. That is the reality: You can pay now or pay later.

In some ways, you feel more organized when you can say, "We're just making a switch from this CEO to that one." But I believe that you're even more organized as a board and appear more conscientious when you don't have the answer yet and admit to that reality. You appear and perform more organized and deliberate as a board when you let the process evolve to give you your answer, and it will give you a better answer.[11]

## Allowing Adequate Time to Change Direction

John Hanson, non-executive chairman and former chief executive officer, Joy Global Inc., a worldwide leader in high-productivity mining solutions, believes the key to success is three-fold: it must be the number one priority of any board, there must be transparency, and it must be allowed to play out over a substantial period of time.

First, the board has to understand not just explicitly but intuitively, that CEO succession planning is its most critical responsibility. If the board truly does understand that intuitively, than it will constantly be working [on] the succession issue and it will see it in the context of a continuum.

Secondly, there needs to be a surprising level of transparency, an openness and honesty in communication, and a sense of accountability on the part of the board. And the third thing is that a succession plan has to span a significant amount of time—I'm thinking three to five years. Without adequate time, it's not only difficult to conduct all the necessary steps in preparation but there's no time to make a mistake—there's no time to change direction. Without these three conditions, it's very hard if not impossible for a board to be effective in the succession process.[12]

## Making Sure the CEO is not Picking a Clone

Manly Molpus, the retired president and chief executive officer, Grocery Manufacturers Association (GMA), considers CEO succession a thorough and successful process if candidates are indentified several years before the transition and given assignments that test their capacity, broaden their experience, and develop their skills.

> My belief is, from what I've seen on the corporate side, you identify the top talent a matter of years back and try to give candidates challenging assignments where they can be measured, but also broader assignments where they can build up their knowledge of the global marketplace and a global company.
>
> Today, you're looking for executives with a broader array of experiences, and it takes more time to try to identify those whom you think can succeed and then give them the opportunity to have some exposure to the board. This level of exposure to the candidates will help ensure that the CEO is not picking a clone who will simply stay the course, but someone who perhaps has a slightly different area of expertise to lead the company through the challenges of a new decade and into greater business opportunities.[13]

## Insisting on Continuous Formal and Informal Contact

Leo Mullin, retired chairman and chief executive officer of Delta Air Lines, Inc., current senior advisor at Goldman Sachs Capital Markets and a director of Johnson & Johnson, believes a critical determinant of success is when the board builds an intimate knowledge of the executive team. Mullin noted that a generation ago, CEO succession planning was far less complicated. In those early years, there was little movement of employees from one company to another. As a result, CEOs and boards knew a great deal about the personalities, talents, and skills of each member of the executive team.

CEO succession planning has always been difficult to conduct but it's become even more difficult to do given the business pressures today compared to just 20 years ago. There's a great deal of luck involved, but a board knows how to create an environment where luck can happen.

> The first step is having the discipline to make it happen. The CEO succession process is most successful when the company has positive stability and can retain and develop its internal talent in an atmosphere of stability. In this environment, it also

becomes important for the board to be extremely knowledgeable of senior management. Board members have to insist on constant formal and informal contact with the executive team.[14]

## Signaling to the Company the Culture that you Value

Raymond Viault, retired vice chairman, General Mills, Inc., and a director of Newell Rubbermaid, believes success in CEO succession is a function of a broader succession plan throughout the company, board awareness of and familiarity with emerging talent, and the ability of a company to sustain its culture. Boards have the ability to shape the company's culture by advancing the candidates who exemplify the right set of attitudes, beliefs, and values.

> I believe it's a big mistake to think you've got a great CEO succession plan if you don't have a more general succession plan for the entire organization. It's not a good way to proceed if the board is suddenly presented with a list of people they don't know who are candidates to run the company. Boards need the opportunity to know who the candidates are and see them perform well before they become candidates.
>
> In my experience, participating in successful successions, the top performers in middle management level and above were always visible to the board. Management makes an effort to identify, career track, and develop the individuals who have the capacity to lead the organization. These high potentials are then put in front of the board on a more regular basis so directors can get comfortable with who the individuals are, how they answer questions, and perform under pressure.
>
> Successful companies take succession planning very seriously. They realize that this is an important part of what an organization is. The people you decide who will move up versus those who don't is the clearest signal you can give to your organization as to what you value. Companies with strong cultures somehow do much better than companies where the culture is driven or changed solely by the guy at the top. Signaling to the company the culture that you value and want to sustain has a very significant effect on how well succession goes.[15]

## EMBRACING THE THIRD RAIL

As we stated earlier, board members are intelligent, business-savvy leaders. They wouldn't have risen to such positions of power and authority without possessing some level of business acumen and a wealth of experience. They express an awareness of the risks inherent in failed CEO succession, yet far too great a percentage continue to treat leadership transition as the third rail of business by deflecting the responsibility, delaying the planning, or avoiding the process altogether.

Succession planning is a challenging and time-consuming process. It may not be considered urgent when compared to other more pressing strategic issues, and the power, ego, legacy, and personal agendas can surely give rise to unwanted emotional stress. However, boards have little choice. The cost of business failure is too high to ignore what is arguably the most critical event in the life of the companies they serve.

Moreover, the cacophony of voices—from shareholders to consumer groups to government regulators—are not abating but becoming more outspoken in their demands for greater board accountability and governance. The bottom line is that boards must find a way to confront their concerns and apprehensions and work through these challenges.

Many of our clients have done just that. They have learned that the only way to control powerful psychological forces and organizational dynamics is by deferring to a disciplined process, understood and accepted by all parties—a process that, by its very presence, neutralizes personal and emotional issues. This is what we've learned in our in-depth interviews—that's it far easier in the long run to deal with the emotions than stumble or fail as an organization.

Every director interviewed has, at one time or another, experienced one or more failures in succession planning. Each now insists that CEO succession planning be an active undertaking, that boards and management work through the emotions, and that a comprehensive process reveal the next dynamic leader. They've accepted the reality, embraced the third rail, and installed a repeatable method for success. They are no longer looking down at the process but up to the opportunity. They are not merely mitigating the cost of failure but benefitting from growth opportunities realized through each leadership transition.

# RHR's Essential Point of View

**4**

*"Policies are many, principles are few. Policies will change, principles never do."*

—John C. Maxwell[1]

RHR's years of business practice, combined with the keen insights of our clients, our ongoing program of research, and our deep understanding of human and organizational behavior, have taught us invaluable lessons—principles that have guided our perspective and helped us establish the best practices in CEO succession planning.

Many boards of directors define success as appointing a successor who meets their qualifications and wins the approval of shareholders and analysts. Though selecting the right CEO is *the* goal and certainly the best gauge of a successful succession process, there are other measures almost as important as picking the right leader that inform the way in which boards approach and manage the entire process. These broader measures not only guide boards in selecting the best possible successor, but also ensure that the company emerges intact, aligned, and stronger from what is a very delicate and nuanced endeavor. They include strengthening alignment among the board and key company executives regarding current and future strategy, retaining and building the talent bench, and maximizing the opportunities inherent in the leadership transition.

## ASSUMPTIONS THAT GUIDE OUR PERSPECTIVE

Nearly 70 years of practice has sharpened our ability to excel in succession planning and broadened our perspective on the mindset directors must have before and throughout the succession process. Boards must not lose sight of the importance of succession planning; when difficulties do arise, no elaborate program or regimented process will make a difference if the board isn't guided by a higher purpose and a pursuit of the best practices in leadership development. There are far too many instances of boards with detailed CEO succession programs failing during the succession process because they have not acknowledged these realities:

## Selecting the CEO is the Board's Most Critical Responsibility, Necessarily Executed in Partnership with the Incumbent CEO

The most important decision any board of directors can make is the selection of the CEO. Getting this decision right will have significant impact on the sustained success of an organization, while getting it wrong will set in motion a ripple effect of adverse consequences. Successful companies are governed by boards that accept full accountability for the CEO succession process and plan for the transitioning of each leader well in advance of the incumbent CEO's departure. A comprehensive succession program includes responsibilities shared by the board, the CEO, and corporate management, but accountability for the entire process rests on the shoulders of the board of directors.

Above and beyond the shared responsibilities and acceptance of accountability, successful CEO successions can only result from a close and on-going partnership between the board and the incumbent CEO. The CEO has perhaps the richest understanding of the context and demands of the position, the day-to-day operations of the enterprise, and the depth of knowledge of each executive team member.

## CEO Succession is a Vital Event in an Organization's History and is *Always* Disruptive

CEO succession is a major systemic transition that causes changes in a company's performance, in the makeup and dynamics of the executive team, in the ways board members relate to one another, and in shareholders' perceptions of the organization.

When there is a change at the top, the organization's vision, strategy, culture, values, and market position are all in play. Unplanned, this disruption can derail the firm if the succession is not managed effectively. Alternately, a well-managed succession can minimize turmoil and, in some instances, initiate purposeful change. A well-planned leadership transition, even with a carefully selected external successor, can create opportunities for innovation and growth, allowing fresh energy, greater vision, and improved planning to energize the organization.

## Psychological Forces will Affect *Every* CEO Succession

The task of transitioning leadership will always be an emotionally charged endeavor. Strong emotions and ego-driven power plays will flare up at all stages of the succession process, making it even more vital that the board's sense of obligation overrides their own subjective opinions and personal gains.

Aware and accepting of this reality, boards have learned that the only way to mitigate the presence and influence of powerful psychological forces is by deferring to a disciplined process that is to be understood and accepted in advance by all parties. This process, by its very presence, neutralizes personal issues and reconciles the many forces at play, and regardless of the difficulties in implementing it, one can rest assured that the consequences of avoiding or hastening the succession process are far greater than the temporary challenges of managing a forceful personality.

It should be noted that emotions are not only at play in the board-room. Effective succession is measured not only be the ability of its board members to overcome personal misgivings, but also by the retention of key executives who may have been passed over, and by how quickly and capably the new executive team regains its best level of performance. A duty-bound board, personifying comportment, cooperation, and fairness during the succession process, can define the culture of the organization and stand as a model of attitude and behavior for the executive team to follow.

## How the Process is Managed will Affect the Reputation of the Company and the Board

There are far too many instances of failed CEO succession planning resulting in the sudden departure or dismissal of the CEO—with no immediate successor prepared to take the reins. In most every instance, the results have been devastating to the company's reputation, reflected in loss of consumer trust, falling market share, and declining stock value.

Moreover, a diminished image is not just external to the organization. How well or poorly the succession process is managed affects the ability of the company to retain its key talent—from executives to new hires. A company's reputation for sound and consistent leadership will affect the ability of the firm to recruit new talent. It will also influence a company's ability to recruit new board members.

Shareholders have become keenly aware of the need for CEO succession planning, and the selection and transitioning of a company's top leader is now one of the most important areas to evaluate when assessing a company's prospectus. Investors and analysts, now more than ever, realize the need for corporate governance and that CEO succession planning depends, in large part, on a sound process originating at the board level.

## The Net Results of the Selection Decision will Not be Fully Determined for Several Years

Directors must acknowledge that the results of their succession decision will not be fully realized until several years after the succession event. This necessary mindset recognizes the difference between short-term expectation, with immediate and somewhat measurable results, and long-term planning, with unforeseen outcomes that may not be known until well into or near the end of the successor's term in office.

The board must hold to the belief that the greater the care and discipline given to the succession process, the more promising the outcome. The board's alignment on the strategic direction of the company will help determine the requisite skills and talents of the successor, while a comprehensive evaluation of candidates will ensure that the company retains its best executive talent—a critical resource the top leader will need in order to achieve and sustain the long-term goals of the company.

## Our 10 Key Dimensions

In the course of our succession planning experience, we have concluded that there are 10 Key Dimensions to effective CEO succession planning. These essential elements—what we consider the ingredients for success—will help any organization build and maintain a successful CEO succession program. Each of these dimensions must be maintained to ensure that the risks inherent in each leadership transition are minimized and the best outcomes are achieved. Having good practices to manage each of these 10 Dimensions in a continuous process will ensure that a board of directors is operating at peak effectiveness and efficiency and that its CEO succession planning program is, without question, a best practice.

## 1. Establish Board Ownership, Involvement, and Oversight

More than at any other time in corporate history, stakeholders now expect a company's board of directors to have a command of the entire CEO succession process—from candidate selection to post-succession evaluation. An explicit, ongoing process for managing CEO succession should be chartered into the board's bylaws with a board committee given explicit oversight duties. Care must be taken that the board not abdicate the responsibility of CEO succession to a sole individual or entity, whether it be the CEO, the chairman, or the search firm. According to recent guidance from the Securities and Exchange Commission, succession planning is now recognized as a fundamental duty of a board of directors and part of the larger risk-management picture, with serious repercussions if planning is not handled correctly.[2] As a result, shareholders are increasingly demanding that boards disclose information about a company's CEO succession plans. In order to stay ahead of this scrutiny, boards must reassure the investment community and the marketplace that it does indeed have an ongoing succession process in place, even if boards elect not to share the kind of specific detail that could harm the company competitively.

Given that CEO succession is a milestone event in a company's history and has the propensity to disrupt the fiscal, operational, and market performance of an organization, there must be active and regular involvement on the part of the board—in partnership with the CEO—in all aspects of succession planning.

We have always believed that a board should be *the* governing body entrusted with full accountability for CEO succession planning, but the real current of understanding must run more deeply than simply acknowledging who owns it and why.

The insight is in knowing how to best navigate the interpersonal dynamics between the board and the CEO and among board members themselves. Over the years, we have discovered that greater success in succession is dependent upon a lead director or non-executive chair who personally orchestrates the way in which board ownership for this process is defined and managed in partnership with the CEO.

## 2. Set Succession Time frames

Regardless of how difficult the activity or unwelcome the task, the board should always be considering and planning for the transitioning of the company's leadership. Boards of directors must ensure that the companies they serve have the ability to sustain excellence in CEO leadership over time with seamless transitions from one leader to the next. Yet, according to our studies, more than half of today's directors don't know when their CEO plans to step down.[3]

Given the complexity of the role of the CEO, comprehensive preparation of internal candidates should begin at least five years in advance of an anticipated transition. A succession conceived and completed in too short a time doesn't allow for a change of direction or recovery from mistakes. For this reason, CEO succession planning must begin immediately following the instatement of a new CEO and be a constant, ongoing process that is managed as closely and attentively as any of the company's critical business issues.

Determining whether and how long the outgoing CEO should remain on the board should be decided on a case-by-case basis. In this regard, several timing aspects must be considered: the expected departure date of the incumbent CEO; the time it takes to develop internal talent for the role; whether (and how long) the outgoing CEO should remain on the board; when to involve a search firm; and the transition time from one CEO to the next. Since boards generally meet only a few times a year, it may be helpful to think of a succession process in terms of the number of board meetings between now and the expected transition rather than in terms of months or years.

## 3. Prepare for Emergencies

An emergency succession plan ensures the continuous coverage of executive duties and safeguards the interests of the company's stakeholders, reputation, and value-creating activities. An emergency succession plan also provides guidelines to the board for temporarily appointing an interim CEO. Yet 40 percent of the directors we surveyed claim that they are not prepared for an emergency succession in the event of a sudden, unexpected, or unplanned departure of their company's top leader.[4]

An absence of leadership is a very dangerous and risky way to manage a business. It's an embarrassing indication of poor board governance, but moreover, it has an immediately detrimental effect on the company's market position and share value.

Boards never know when they may have to implement an emergency CEO succession due to an unexpected leadership void. For this reason, boards should always be thinking about and planning for succession. When a company is blindsided by the sudden departure (or loss in tragic circumstances) of its CEO, boards must react immediately, though calmly and decisively. They must assure the public, customers, and employees that new leadership will soon be in place, either permanently or on an interim basis.

## 4. Align on Strategy and Profile

CEO succession is a milestone event that can affect an organization's vision, values, culture, strategy, and market value. A well-strategized CEO succession plan can minimize turmoil, initiate purposeful change, and create opportunities for innovation and growth. Conversely, without thorough planning, the disruption caused by a change in CEOs can defocus and derail an organization.

The board must align on two aspects 1) on the strategic direction of the company, and 2) on the requisite capabilities to lead the company into that strategic future. If the board is not aligned on the first it will have even greater difficulty agreeing on the second.

Before discussing prospective candidates, it's vital for the board to determine the current market position of the company, its collective vision and direction for the future, and the strategy and culture required to achieve its near-term and long-term goals. Political dynamics and competing agendas, often unacknowledged, are significant impediments that can derail or misdirect the board. We've seen competing agendas lead to hastily or poorly chosen successors, regardless of how buttoned up a board's succession planning program may have been.

The full context of what is needed in the next CEO must be derived from solid, broad-based information that has been vigorously and openly discussed among, and agreed to by, every board member. Once the criteria are clear and relevant, discussions of candidates— compared to the strategic criteria—will be more meaningful and systematic.

Candor, intellectual honesty, and congeniality are imperative, for if the process is disorganized or divisive, highly talented candidates may "opt out" before the selection decision is made and non-candidates, who are otherwise key players on the executive team, may leave the company, driven by a sense of unfairness or a fear of strategic misdirection.

## 5. Build the Talent Pipeline

Sixty-seven percent of the directors we surveyed indicated that the biggest challenge to CEO succession is a shortage of candidates.[5] In our practice, we find that the perception of too few candidates is the result of not approaching succession planning as an ongoing process that requires the continuous and challenging development of potential successors.

Creating a culture of development, not just among the executive team, but two or three levels deep into the organization, sustains a company's performance at all levels, and ensures the retention of key talent. It will most certainly create an environment that nurtures the development and surfacing of capable leaders. Even if the board goes outside the organization to select the next CEO, a corporate culture that identifies and develops its talent is more likely to have committed, effective, trusting employees at all levels of the organization. With the development of a leadership pipeline, the executive team ought to be more accepting of the new leader, for each will have had a chance to audition for the role.

In a corporate culture void of development, an unplanned departure of a CEO will always force a sudden and superficial assessment of executive talent, prompt an external search, and provoke a competitive, untrusting environment from which an unprepared CEO will most likely emerge—and most likely be rejected.

Regular discussions and reviews of a prospective talent pool two to three levels deep within the organization must occur, and candidates provided a customized development program with challenging assignments. These assignments must be meaningful and bear a real risk of failure in order to allow the board a full view of what each candidate is capable of accomplishing under pressure.

Careful cultivation of talent and a fair evaluation process can also help retain candidates who may be unsuitable for the role of CEO, but are strong performers nevertheless, and critical to the ongoing success of the company.

## 6. Source External Talent and Manage Search Firms

External candidates, if part of the succession planning program, must be identified and their career paths monitored for successes and failures against circumstances and events in their own company and industry. Although boards may not have the capabilities to identify and monitor qualified, accessible external talent, input from search firms can provide valuable information about viable candidates. To benefit the most from their expertise, search firms will be most valuable in identifying appropriate external candidates when they thoroughly understand the requesting company's culture, the alignment of its board, and the company's strategic direction.

Care must always be taken when hiring external talent. An externally hired CEO's annual compensation can be 75 to 100 percent greater than that of an internal appointment. In addition, an outside CEO is less likely to stay long term and has a higher risk of early failure.[6] These are not the only risks. The high cost and short tenure of an externally hired CEO can upset confidence in the board and throughout the company. Stock prices can be negatively affected and key people may leave the organization, leading to further reliance on external talent and maintaining a cycle of failed successions.

While an experienced search consultant can help identify qualified external candidates, the search firm cannot be allowed to take over the process; its role is to guide and facilitate the process on behalf of the board. It's ultimately the board's responsibility to select the proper candidate from the slate of internal and external talent.

In addition to identifying and qualifying external candidates, search firms can serve as a fair witness and facilitator to the board during critical stages of the succession planning process by assessing internal talent, ensuring objectivity, maintaining transparency, mitigating emotionally charged issues, and benchmarking best practices from other organizations.

## 7. Select the CEO

Because of the critical opportunity afforded a company when making the right decision, and the immeasurable cost for getting it wrong, the CEO selection decision must be grounded in a thorough and in-depth assessment of each candidate. The foundational guide for this entire assessment process is the Leader Profile, the blueprint that defines the requisite leadership skills and character traits expected of the successor CEO.

Boards need insightful information on, and meaningful interactions with, each prospect. Candidate assessments should examine the nominee's knowledge, skills, competencies, social intelligence, and other personal attributes in order to form a broad picture of each candidate's capabilities and potential. Presentations alone by candidates are not adequate, nor are resumes or letters of praise. The fact that 60 percent of board members rate themselves as having inadequate interviewing skills suggests the need for a deeper analysis of candidates from unbiased individuals who are independent of the search process.[7]

Given the difficulty of knowing what skills will be most important in the future, integrity, trustworthiness, and sound character are critical attributes that transcend any situation. Stable characteristics such as personality and cognitive abilities are not readily identified in interviews, but need to be taken into account and can be gauged accurately through a professional assessment procedure.

## 8. Proactively Manage the Transition

We believe the events surrounding a transition of leadership fall into two stages: stage one begins the moment the succession decision is made and ends when the incumbent CEO transfers leadership to the new CEO; stage two is marked by that first day of the new CEO's term of office.

These stages are so closely aligned and necessarily seamless that we feel it best to address this continuum from "hands off" to "hands on" as one chapter in our book to emphasize the continuity and entirety of that process.

Too often, CEO succession is viewed as an event rather than a process. As a result, the needs, wisdom, and experience of the outgoing leader are not always leveraged and shared with the new CEO. This can potentially lead to a misalignment between the incoming CEO and the board, and this disorganization has the potential to cause strategic disconnections between the new CEO and the company's executive team. Well-managed successions allow time for the outgoing CEO to transition his or her vision and knowledge of the company as well as the profiles of the executive team to the incoming CEO. Allowing time for the transitioning of knowledge is clearly critical to maintaining business continuity.

Our research indicates that 41 percent of directors do not believe they pay sufficient attention to either the integration of a new CEO with the board or to the strategic differences that might arise between the new CEO and board.[8] This lack of integration is easily one of the greatest reasons for short, unsuccessful tenures and the high rate of CEO failures—many within the first year of a new CEO's term.[9]

Once the successor is named and in place, it is tempting for the board to breathe a sigh of relief and feel that the transition process is completed. However, contrary to current opinion, the process of integration is more complex than originally thought, given the greater complexity of business, and takes much longer than the traditional three-month "honeymoon" period usually allowed by most organizations. While the first 100 days are critical, a CEO's integration does not stop at that point. Current research shows that successful integration actually takes between 12 and 18 months.[10]

## 9. Measure Performance and Improve Process

After the new CEO is selected and the transition from the outgoing CEO to the incoming CEO is completed, the board needs to attend to two more important tasks. The first of these is gauging how well the new CEO is performing in the critical first year. The second is to conduct a review of the actual succession process. The first of these tasks is critical to identify any early indicators of problems that need to be addressed early in the new CEO's term of office. The second provides the opportunity to capture lessons learned while they are still fresh and to make adjustments in the CEO succession process.

Every CEO succession faced by a company will bring new situations, challenges, and issues to bear. And each new CEO will usher in new personalities and behaviors, new business dynamics, and new human relations and interactions. For these reasons, every succession brings new knowledge and discoveries that must be added to the board's governance memory. This is an important concept, for the board members who were involved in the preceding succession may not be involved in the next succession. In that five to seven year time frame, the makeup of the board could change dramatically.

We believe the most constructive position to take is for boards and CEOs to view measuring performance as a partnership where the board and CEO come together to tackle issues and collaborate on solutions for the success of the organization. With this mindset, engaging in regular and professional reviews of expectations and performance should strengthen, not strain, the relationship between the board and the CEO.

Within the first year of a new CEO's term of office, the board should assess every step of the leadership development and succession planning process to highlight those procedures that effectively and efficiently resulted in the selection of the current CEO and are worth repeating. The board will also want to identify process problems that detracted from best practice and figure out how to correct each issue.

A candid review of the entire CEO succession process must attend every leadership transition event and include key stakeholder input. Observations and decisions made during the process should be chronicled for future reference. After each succession cycle, the steps taken in the succession process should be discussed, evaluated, and calibrated to encourage continuous learning and improvement of the succession program and the board's methodology. If changes to a committee charter or any components of the succession process need to be made, they should reflect what has been learned and should be incorporated before the lessons fade.

## 10. Managing the Dynamics in CEO Succession

CEO succession is far more than the transitioning of a company's leadership; it is a process fundamental to the sustained success of a company. Moreover, a successful succession outcome is the product of a partnership between the board of directors and the CEO, making ongoing communication and alignment between the board and the CEO essential.

The only path to this successful outcome is for boards and CEOs to openly and authentically work together in all aspects of CEO succession planning—from aligning on strategy and purpose, to continuously cultivating a talent pipeline of leaders for all levels of the organization, to facilitating an effortless transition of leadership.

Therefore, while each of the previous nine dimensions to effective CEO succession planning defines a specific stage in the succession process with identifiable tasks and outcomes, this tenth and final dimension addresses the relational dynamics among the various players involved in each stage of the process.

Moreover, this tenth dimension speaks to the personal emotions and challenges that have a direct bearing on the thoughts and actions of the executives involved, affecting how they view themselves and their relationship with their peers and superiors. These driving, often conflicting forces of ego, position power, fear, and uncertainty seldom rise above the surface in business. Yet they add a layer of complexity when left unresolved or only shared in private with a spouse, close friend, or mentor.

Our point of view is that boards and CEOs can be far more productive and successful if these emotions are openly acknowledged and resolved. By effectively managing the personal feelings that will always well up during succession planning, stakeholders can channel their experiences and energy into a powerful, productive force for the benefit of the organization, and ultimately, themselves.

## Learning from History

The business environment has endured tremendous change over the past several decades, the intensity of which has had a profound effect on CEO succession planning. Clearly, the mindset of directors and their approach to leadership transition, in just the past 20 years alone, can no longer guarantee success in this accelerated global age. The process of CEO selection and succession has become far more involved and the repercussions of success or failure, far more consequential.

The best boards are using the insights and lessons from their own experiences—as well as witnessing the adversity of their peers—to avoid repeating the CEO succession failures of the past. They have learned that the only way to safeguard business continuity is by sustaining the organization's leadership, with seamless transitions from one carefully appointed chief executive to the next, and with each succeeding leader thoroughly prepared to take the company further and higher than the last.

The core tenet of our point of view is that CEO succession planning is far more than the transitioning of a company's leadership; it is fundamental to the success or failure of a company. When effectively and comprehensively executed, CEO succession planning can ensure the progression and advancement of a company's strategic direction, create new opportunities for its growth, ensure the continuity of its culture, and safeguard the retention and development of its talent.

In Part II, we will explore each of the 10 Key Dimensions in detail including a description of the parameters of each dimension and the methodologies that will help boards systemize each dimension as a best practice within the culture and operations of the organization.

# PART II

# THE 10 KEY DIMENSIONS OF EFFECTIVE SUCCESSION

Over the course of our near seven decades of succession-planning experience, we have identified 10 Key Dimensions to effective CEO succession planning, and the essential steps within each that must be comprehensively managed to ensure that the risks inherent in CEO succession are minimized and the best outcomes achieved.

In addition to defining the essential steps in developing, selecting, and transitioning a company's leadership, we explore the relational dynamics among board members and between the board and the CEO that attend every phase of the process. We also examine the personal emotions that sway and influence even the most experienced executives—an often-overlooked aspect of the success or failure of the succession process.

CEO succession is more than a board's responsibility. Although the board is accountable for the process, we strongly believe that there must be a partnership between board and CEO—a partnership built on personal authenticity and trust. Best practice can only be achieved when board and CEO reach an understanding of involvement—a division of labor orchestrated by the board and adhered to by both parties.

*"I decided when I was going to move into this role, and I'll decide when I'm going to leave it!"*

—An anonymous, short-tenured
CEO of a *Fortune* 500 company

Of the Ten Key Dimensions to effective CEO succession planning, Board Ownership, Involvement, and Oversight is necessarily the first element. This first dimension establishes and defines the fundamental mindset of the board, the one body that is in the best position to safeguard the continuity of the corporation by ensuring its sound leadership.

## A DEEPER CURRENT OF UNDERSTANDING

Over the past 10 years, many external voices—including shareholders, analysts, regulators, and consumer groups—have stepped up their rhetoric, insisting on greater corporate governance and regulation, and that boards be accountable for the entire CEO succession planning and selection process.

Considering the corporate accounting scandals at the onset of the twenty-first century to the collapse of the financial markets in 2007, should we have expected investors and other stakeholders to react any differently?

Given all that's transpired during this past decade, there is hardly a director nowadays that doesn't understand and accept the responsibility for succession planning. Directors get it, but despite their awareness, there still exists a lack of knowledge and a wide variation of skills, comfort, and experience with the process.

A far greater obstacle, though, is directors' ambivalence in asserting their responsibility and ownership—an uncertainty that stems from a host of psychological forces and organizational dynamics that vex even the most experienced. Directors are reluctant to force the issue of succession, particularly if the company has an assertive leader with an attitude similar to the anonymous CEO quoted at the beginning of this chapter.

Directors want to maintain a good rapport with their CEO. They also want to hold on to their board seat for all the personal and professional reasons people want to serve on boards. It becomes understandable, then, that board members will not risk conflicts with their CEO or the board chair, who in many companies are one and the same. Thus directors will back away from the issue and allow CEO succession to recede to the back burner for another quarter, or the following year. For these and so many other reasons, CEO succession planning seldom, if ever, runs as smoothly as it should or could.

We have always believed that a board should be *the* governing body entrusted with full accountability for CEO succession planning, but the real current of understanding must run more deeply than simply acknowledging who owns it and why.

The insight lies in knowing how to best navigate the interpersonal dynamics between the board and the CEO and among board members themselves. Over the years, we've discovered that greater success in succession is dependent upon a lead director or non-executive chair who personally orchestrates the way in which board ownership is defined and managed in partnership with the CEO.

In addition to a lead director with the sound judgment and relational skills necessary to negotiate the difficult terrain of personality conflicts and emotions, there are other insights that help board members find a more confident, steadier voice when asserting their governance. For regardless as to how challenging the succession process may be, at the end of the day, the board is still charged with its legal and fiduciary responsibility to ensure the overall management and supervision of the corporation.

## Living with the Choice

CEOs, setting out to achieve specific objectives during their time in office, will pick the key officers most capable of helping them reach those goals. It's their responsibility to hire the individuals they believe possess the talents and skills to make things happen. Aside from selecting officers with business and financial acumen, CEOs also choose their executive team for character and personality fit—individuals they can openly communicate with and place their trust in.

A board of directors has the same level of responsibility, and on behalf of all internal and external stakeholders, is duty-bound to hire a CEO who can deliver against the strategic plan, and with whom they can place their confidence and trust. A CEO who insists on selecting the successor as a "last act" before leaving office is, in reality, hamstringing the board by forcing the directors to accept his or her choice for what is undoubtedly the most important personnel decision in the entire company.

Such a decision could unfairly restrict a board looking to alter the strategic direction of the company while the outgoing CEO may have intentionally picked a successor to maintain the status quo. It could also serve to frustrate directors forced to work with a CEO whose personality doesn't necessarily blend well with the chemistry of the board.

Weighing the temporary, emotional pitfalls involved in selecting a successor against five to ten years of having to live and work with a powerful person who is not of their choosing may make directors think twice before deferring the selection decision to the outgoing CEO.

## Restraint of Power

As Lord Acton once observed, "Power tends to corrupt, and absolute power corrupts absolutely."[1] Ambition, greed, and hubris are all human conditions, and all are aggravated by power. And power, when unchecked, has the potential to misguide the intentions of any person at any station in life.

Domineering CEOs may have difficulty distinguishing between personal ambition and the needs of the corporation, and when driven by excessive ego and pride, may be reluctant to step aside when the time comes. We've noticed that this assertive attitude is more prevalent in instances where the board did not hire the CEO—but the outgoing leader did. A successor who is selected and empowered by the outgoing CEO may believe that he or she is not fully accountable to the board, or need not be strategically aligned with the board on any or all business decisions. And this can become even more untenable when the outgoing CEO stays on as the board chair.

Between external stakeholders demanding greater accountability and the emotional tensions and personality conflicts that surface when planning and executing the transitioning of a leader, boards of directors are finding themselves stuck between the proverbial rock and a hard place. Their reluctance and frustrations become understandable, but they have no choice: they must own and drive the CEO succession planning process. What they do have are solutions. There is a model for success in governance.

## It Goes Beyond Charter

Best practice today suggests that boards establish a committee explicitly chartered with the responsibility for driving the CEO succession planning process and for frequently updating all directors on its progress. The presence of a formal committee chartered with succession planning sends an important message to the CEO, executive team, employees, shareowners, and other stakeholders that succession planning will be a disciplined, objective, and ongoing business practice.

Medium to large-size boards will often appoint a Governance and Nominating Committee or Compensation Committee, while smaller boards will approach CEO selection as a committee of the whole. Some boards prefer a less formal, more ad hoc approach, creating instead a "task force" of interested directors. The danger with this approach is that an informal, unchartered task force may be perceived as being too casual and undisciplined on the one hand, or too secretive and agenda-driven on the other, potentially creating even greater anxiety and feelings of mistrust in the CEO and among the executive team.

Without question, we advise appointing a chartered committee, but this is standard operating procedure nowadays for most *Fortune* 500 companies, especially given the succession issues of the last few years. The deeper insight is in the scope of that charter and how it is actually exercised. Also, since every board member will have to live with the CEO succession decision, every board member should have a hand in the selection and be comfortable with that decision.

## An Integrated Leadership Development Plan

Many boards do not bring up CEO succession as an agenda item in the quarterly or bi-monthly meetings unless there's an imminent succession date. The problem is, when CEO succession is viewed as narrowly as replacing a CEO who isn't functioning well or is expected to retire, it winds up becoming an event-driven incident that only receives attention when there's a pressing, unavoidable need.

A generation or two ago, impromptu planning and eleventh-hour decision-making may have been sufficient. But against the backdrop of today's constantly shifting business landscape, boards planning and deciding a few months out who will lead the company forward is not nearly dynamic enough to safeguard the strategic direction and sustained success of the company.

The best approach is to have CEO succession embedded within the corporation's full leadership succession and leadership development agenda. In this manner, the board will have, in its governance charter, the responsibility for ensuring the appropriate development and succession of all officer roles. The outcome is continuity planning and appraisal for all officer positions, including that of the CEO.

The reality is that CEO succession is not simply transitioning of the top leader, but an ongoing, multi-year process that, when involving an internal successor, will most likely require the orchestration of other moves two or three levels deep within the organization. For example, if the CFO is selected to become the CEO, then the company will require a new chief financial officer—possibly the company's controller or treasurer, or someone outside the organization. Any of these moves, as in a chess game, requires interdependent, sequential maneuvers that must be planned out well in advance of the date of transition, with all candidates undergoing continuous development and assessment.

A best practice for boards is to champion performance management throughout the organization by advocating the development and assessment of all company executives on a regular basis. This requires boards to have, in the charter of one of its committees, the oversight of all management and leadership development, purposely to ensure that the company has the talent—at all leadership levels— to achieve its near- and long-term objectives.

Leo Mullin, former CEO of Delta Airlines and director of Johnson & Johnson, considers CEO succession planning as an opportunity for the board to influence the performance and future direction of the organization and, for that reason, insists that elements of strategic alignment and executive development be discussed at every board meeting.

> For us, succession planning is a never-ending process that continuously identifies and develops talent two to three levels deep within our company. We want to ensure that the development plans for all our officers and their successors are always aligned to our strategic goals. This includes the CEO and his potential successors. Our ongoing preference as a board is to find an internal successor to the CEO in order to maintain our strategic heading and preserve our culture.
>
> The board's succession planning committee works closely with the sitting CEO and HR to profile and evaluate candidates against a constantly shifting strategic horizon. We test candidates, evaluate their performance, and have rotated formal meetings with potential successors. For us, a well-defined succession process with clearly articulated responsibilities between the board and management, planned out three to five years in advance for all officers, is our model for success and an assurance of continuity in leadership, whether planned or unplanned.[2]

## CONTINUOUS DEVELOPMENT AND APPRAISAL

Best practice suggests the use of a profile or The Winning Formula that defines the leadership requirements, characteristics, and capabilities of the CEO and all officer positions. These profiles should be appraised periodically and tie back into the development of the candidates, including the development and appraisal of the CEO.

The board should always be attentive to the continuous development of the company's top leadership. If a company has a 52-year-old incumbent who isn't planning to retire for another five to seven years, the board should encourage that CEO to continuously update his or her knowledge base in order to keep ahead of new markets, competitors, or technologies.

## A PARTNERSHIP BUILT ON TRUST

As we noted earlier, directors, over the past several years, have grown in their understanding of their role in succession planning, but we've also discovered that powerful personalities and organizational dynamics have resulted in directors expressing a range of opinion—from apprehensive to hard-boiled—about who should lead the CEO succession planning process.

At one end of the continuum are those who defer succession planning and selection to the CEO. They concede that the CEO knows best the company's business strategy and operations, has day-to-day familiarity with each member of the executive team, and has the best idea which of those direct reports will make the ideal successor. In our recent survey, inclusive of planning, selection, and integration, 48 percent of directors state that the responsibility for selection and succession belongs to the CEO.[3]

On the other end of the continuum are directors who believe candidate selection and succession is the board's sole responsibility. They contend that the CEO may show bias or short-sightedness and may choose a successor not aligned with the company's strategic future but with the status quo. Some fear that the CEO may be unwilling to step down altogether, or do so at some unplanned time. For these and a host of other reasons, many directors on this end of the spectrum prefer to leave the CEO out of the succession process altogether.

Our point of view is that there must be a partnership between the board and the CEO on succession planning—a partnership built on trust and a common objective to sustain the long term success of the enterprise. Just as the board and CEO work together in managing the strategy, operations, and finances of the company, so too must they work together in ensuring the smooth transitioning of the company's leadership. Unless the CEO is underperforming or has lost the trust and confidence of the directors, planning and collaborating on succession issues is best accomplished with the CEO's input and perspective.

Best practice is achieved when the board and CEO reach an understanding of involvement—a division of labor orchestrated by the board and adhered to by both parties. Since the board will be living with the selection decision long after the sitting CEO has stepped down, it's in the board's best interest to ensure that the entire process is managed collaboratively.

Donald James, chairman and CEO, Vulcan Materials Company, and lead director of Southern Company, agrees that the board and the sitting CEO need to approach the succession planning process in unison. James's belief is that there is an invaluable contribution of ground-level knowledge inherent in the CEO's position—from understanding the strategic challenges and opportunities facing the business to having the knowledge of the operational resources and internal talent capable of meeting those challenges.

There's a tendency for boards today to believe that the sitting CEO should not be involved at all in succession planning. I believe that if the CEO is well-regarded by the board and has been successful in his or her tenure, it's a mistake to exclude the CEO from the process. The board and the company stand to lose a lot of intelligence and guidance if you have a CEO who's committed to the company and not to his or her particular agenda. Probably nobody understands the requirements of the job better than the existing CEO. And he or she is in the position to know which internal candidates are best suited to step into that position over the course of the next three to five years. The CEO will also know what assignments are most appropriate for the testing and development of internal candidates.[4]

## SKILLFUL NAVIGATION

The incumbent CEO will always have a personal interest in his or her successor, either for reasons of legacy or because the CEO has a financially vested interest in how the company will be led. In some circumstances, a large part of the outgoing CEO's net worth may still be tied up in company stock. A handpicked successor may be the outgoing CEO's way of maintaining the status quo of the company, to continue his or her legacy, or protect personal wealth.

In past decades and particularly in smaller companies, the CEO selecting his or her successor was pretty much expected. The CEO led and dominated the succession process—from choosing the successor to deciding when that transition would take place. Even today, there's a natural tendency for boards to defer to the CEO, especially when they are a powerful, influential, long-standing leader who knows the company, its personnel, its operations, and its markets. This is even more the case when the CEO is also the chairperson.

CEOs, who also serve as board chairs, tend to invite associates, friends, even relatives, to sit on their board, individuals who may be inclined to be overly differential to the CEO. In these instances, when the CEO states, "I'm on top of finding my replacement, I have a couple of people in the company that I'm developing," it becomes very difficult for directors to ask to be involved or challenge the CEO's decisions.

It is one thing to claim that partnership between board and CEO is the best solution; it's quite another to know how to skillfully navigate difficult conversations with a powerful CEO and reach agreement on the areas of partnership. When facing a powerful personality, directors have to find a way to convey that although they have great trust and respect for the CEO's candidate selection, they should be involved as well, for at the end of the day, the board will have to work with the successor long after the incumbent leaves office.

## THE ROLE OF THE LEAD DIRECTOR

Stepping down from office is a highly personal and emotionally charged event in the career of a CEO. It's very difficult for a leader—regardless of how powerful and confident that leader may appear to be—to hand over the reins of their company to someone who may not be of their choosing, especially when the sitting CEO's vision is not yet fully realized. Concerns over the continued growth and well-being of the enterprise—not to mention the fear that their own legacy could be disrupted by their successor—can haunt CEOs through to their last days. As the end of their term approaches—sometimes as much as a year out—their sense of fulfillment and accomplishment is often eclipsed by feelings of regret and inadequacy.

In the midst of all of this emotional turmoil, dealing with a board that is pressing to move forward with succession planning is a wrenching, unwanted reality for a CEO, complicated further for the CEO and the board when the CEO is the board chair. In this stressful environment, a non-executive lead director that the CEO can confide in and forge a trusting partnership with, can become an invaluable linchpin between the CEO and the board.

It's a model for success when a CEO can openly share expectations, concerns, and even fears with a lead director and trust that he or she is entering into a confiding partnership with a fair yet empathetic colleague. It takes a perceptive individual with strong relational skills to be that calming force during a difficult chapter in the career of a CEO and to lessen that CEO's fears of being overpowered by the board's ownership of the succession process.

The key insight here is the presence and involvement of an emotionally intelligent lead director who has in his or her arsenal, three critical traits:

- *Principled Judgment*—to make considered decisions by recognizing and assessing situations, incorporating prior experiences, and with confidence and balance, deciding on the best approach while motivated by the long-term best interests of the company.
- *Keen Insight*—to gain an accurate and intuitive understanding of a person or situation and to read, comprehend, and react intelligently to all the dynamics underlying the emotions at play.

- *Fair Wisdom*—to bring together judgment and insight, to make the best use of knowledge and experience and determine what is moral and fair, and to stand by that decision with integrity.

## One of the More Sensitive Issues

Even though the board delegates to the CEO the responsibility of identifying and developing potential successors, the board plays an important role in getting to know the internal candidates and assisting in their cultivation. This is another very sensitive area of involvement for the board as most CEOs understandably do not like the idea of their boss—the board of directors—talking directly to the leader's subordinates.

The issue is even further complicated when this personal contact involves individuals who are not direct reports to the CEO, yet show promise as potential candidates three to five years out. In these instances, having board members spend formal and informal time with non-direct reports, let alone direct reports, can create situations where board members may hear critical comments about the company's leadership. Under these necessary circumstances, it takes a strong and confident CEO to allow unfettered, unmanaged contact of direct and indirect reports with board members.

In order for directors to make a thoroughly informed selection decision, they must have first-hand knowledge of the talents and skills of the candidates and not just rely on reports offered by the CEO. Therefore, a key (and challenging) part of the board's responsibility is to interact with candidates directly, and the evaluation process must specify how and when this interplay will take place.

Candidates should meet with board members as often as time and situations allow, from formal discussions with depth and strategic significance, to informal social events such as dinners, golf outings, and other activities. This way, directors can assess both the business acumen and social intelligence of each potential successor.

Additionally, while it's important to evaluate candidates in a variety of settings, it is equally as important to get to know them over a period of time. Over the course of several meetings, the formality that initially exists between candidates and directors will slowly diminish, ultimately giving directors a more accurate picture of each candidate's unvarnished strengths and weaknesses.

Peter Fasolo, chief human resource officer at Johnson & Johnson, has been involved in a number of successions, having worked with both CEOs and boards while chief talent officer at Kohlberg Kravis Roberts & Company (KKR). Over the years, Fasolo has recognized the need for board members to get to know the candidates personally.

> I do not think, in my personal view, that it's the CEO's job exclusively to pick his or her successor. I strongly believe it falls entirely on the shoulders of the board of directors to make that decision. And if you accept that assumption, then what the board needs to do is to formulate an independent and objective view of each candidate in order to confidently pick the successor. If not, then the board is allowing the CEO to determine his or her own successor and I think that is very dangerous.
>
> The board has to know each of the individuals, their performance track record, their long-term potential, and any issues that may detract from their record of achievements. The board must get to know these candidates on a one-on-one basis in business settings, through presentations and strategy sessions, as well as informally. Ultimately, the directors will be working with the new CEO, so they may as well pick someone they both trust and enjoy working with.[5]

## THE ART OF PREEMPTIVE COMMUNICATION

In 2009, the Security and Exchange Commission made it abundantly clear that there would be consequences if boards of directors failed to include CEO succession plans in their risk portfolios and proposals to shareholders.[6]

Crises tend to bring about change and the recession of 2008, caused, in large part, by the failure of the banking system, prompted the SEC to compel boards to show greater accountability in identifying and preparing CEO successors. That regulatory body could not ignore the level of outrage expressed by investors and consumer activists when the marketplace discovered that Bank of America would be leaderless upon the retirement of its CEO, Ken Lewis.

How well directors handle succession has become a test of board competency by the investment community with shareholders today challenging boards of directors to reveal their CEO succession plans. In order to stay ahead of this scrutiny, boards must reassure shareowners, analysts, regulators, and other stakeholders that it does indeed have a succession process in place, even if the board elects not to share the kind of specific detail that could harm the company competitively.

## A LESSON FROM APPLE

One of the earliest and most visible tests of the new SEC guidance came in February 2011, on the heels of Apple CEO Steve Jobs' announcement of an indefinite medical leave from the company. Central Laborers Pension Fund, a union in Jacksonville, Illinois introduced a proposal that called for Apple's board to spell out its criteria for choosing the next CEO and name internal candidates for the job. CLPF also demanded that Apple begin a "non-emergency CEO succession planning" process and report on it to shareholders each year.

That same February at Apple's annual shareholders meeting, Apple's board advanced a proxy statement making the case why the company's board opposed a public succession plan demanded in the union's proposal[7]:

- The Company's Corporate Governance Guidelines already require the Board and CEO to conduct an annual review of succession planning for senior management, including the CEO. This has been in the board's charter since 1997.
- Disclosing such a succession plan "would give the Company's competitors an unfair advantage for it would publicize the Company's confidential objectives and plans."
- The disclosure would "undermine the Company's efforts to recruit and retain executives. The Board believes that the Company's success depends on attracting and retaining a superior executive team, including the CEO. The disclosure proposal requires a report identifying the candidates being considered for CEO, as well as the criteria used to evaluate each

candidate. Publicly naming these potential successors invites competitors to recruit high-value executives away from Apple. Furthermore, executives who are not identified as potential successors may choose to voluntarily leave the Company."

- Lastly, the disclosure proposal "attempts to micro-manage and constrain the actions of the Board."

Put to a vote, shareowners followed the recommendation of the board and overwhelmingly rejected the succession disclosure proposal by a vote of 400 million to 172 million.[8]

Regardless of this outcome, many individuals including shareowners (albeit a minority), government regulators, the media, and activist consumer groups believe boards should divulge everything they know about CEO succession planning for the companies they serve, including time frames, candidates, and compensation. These demands on the part of these groups are naïve to say the least.

In addition to the points made by Apple's board, Steve Jobs' image is inextricably linked to the brand value of Apple, much like the personas of Berkshire Hathaway's Warren Buffett or Microsoft's Bill Gates. Identifying a most-likely successor might indicate that Jobs might leave inside of two years which could prove potentially damaging to the brand and reputation of the company before Jobs and the board has a chance to establish the credibility of and trust in his successor.

Shareowners, when presented with the implications and dangers of such detailed disclosure will, by and large, vote not to disclose, but that outcome cannot be guaranteed in the future. Nor can boards be assured that regulators won't step up their efforts to force the hands of boards and the companies they serve. That's not to say that shareowners don't want to know or deserve to know that the companies they've invested in have a succession plan in place. That's not what we're suggesting.

Boards would be wise to stay ahead of investors and other constituents by speaking confidently and competently about their preparedness for succession—whether that transition is planned or unplanned. If directors want to control the agenda and minimize external pressures and involvement, they must take every effort to be preemptive in their communications. Boards must give shareowners the confidence that it is informed and has a succession process in place, that candidates are continuously in development, and that the talents and skills of these candidates are aligned to the strategic direction of the organization.

## Oversight of Management and of Self

The board has an oversight responsibility to ensure that all of the shared responsibilities defined in this chapter are managed to the utmost level of professionalism. There is an accountability that the CEO has to the board, but there is also a responsibility that the board has to its shareholders. And the only way to achieve that level of accountability is by board members standing together, duty-bound to each other.

Earlier we spoke of restraint of power. A board's objective, independent oversight helps ensure that the CEO is not overbearing or shirking his or her responsibility, and is placing the needs of the organization above personal interests. The board's oversight involves making certain that the CEO aligns with the strategic direction of the corporation, is objective in candidate selection and development, abides by the defined term of office, and fully shares his or her knowledge and support with the incoming CEO.

Restraint of power and oversight extends to the board itself. Directors are accountable to each other to approach succession planning with objectivity and mission focus. Even if a committee is tasked with the CEO succession plan and process, each board member is responsible for the final decision. Each director must take part in the fair and thorough evaluation of candidates to ensure that the successor has the requisite talents and skills to carry the company into its strategic future.

In addition to being responsible for CEO succession, boards should provide oversight and support for the wider management succession process. Boards often develop relationships with as many as the top twenty or so senior executives within the organization over a period of years. But looking beyond this top layer of senior management, board members may not be familiar with individual company officers. Nevertheless, directors should review the company's leadership development program to ensure that this program is working satisfactorily and producing future leaders—at all levels of the organization.

## Key Insights

✓ Success in CEO succession planning is dependent upon a lead director or non-executive chair who personally orchestrates the way in which board ownership of the succession planning process is defined and managed—in partnership with the CEO.

✓ Just as CEOs have the responsibility to select direct reports who will help them achieve their goals while in office, so too must boards by selecting their direct report—the CEO. It's the board's legal and fiduciary responsibility to choose a capable leader who can work with the board and deliver against the strategic plan of the corporation.

✓ The board should have, in its governance charter, the responsibility for ensuring the appropriate development and succession of all officer roles. The outcome is continuity planning for all officer positions, including that of the CEO.

✓ The CEO and board must work together toward a successful succession. The CEO knows the business and the talent of the executive team, and must be part of the process. The CEO must also help in the transitioning of his or her successor to ensure transfer of knowledge and business continuity.

✓ If directors want to control the agenda and minimize external involvement and regulatory pressures, they must take every effort to be preemptive in their communications. Boards must give shareowners the confidence that it has a succession process in place, that candidates are continuously in development, and that the talents and skills of these candidates are aligned to the strategic direction of the organization.

# SET SUCCESSION TIME FRAMES

# 6

"Companies that have strong cultures oriented toward minding the store over long periods of time seem to be the ones who have the least controversial and better thought through successions. Those dominated by whoever is running it at the top are the ones that have the problems."
—Raymond Viault, former vice chairman, General Mills, and independent director of Newell Rubbermaid, and VF Corporation

## THE CONSIDERATION OF TIMING AS A BEST PRACTICE

In the absence of a looming succession date or of a sudden unplanned departure or dismissal, there is a natural tendency for boards to treat CEO succession as an episodic event set to occur somewhere in the distant future.

The incumbent CEO may be a young, healthy leader, performing very well in office, and may be five or more years from expected retirement. Taking up the issue of succession early in such a leader's tenure may imply a lack of confidence in the young CEO, provoking feelings of inadequacy, and maybe even prompting an unplanned departure.

It could also create a horserace among internal succession candidates or cause an exodus of key talent not under consideration. Not wanting to needlessly "tweak" such strong emotions or devote board time to non-critical-path issues, directors will gladly shift their attention to more pressing agenda items, whether it is an acquisition, expanding into another international market, or selling off a line of business.

For these and other psychological and organizational reasons, most boards tend to defer thinking about CEO succession until a transition date is imminent—usually within 12 to 18 months of the sitting CEO's retirement. But to approach the entirety of leadership succession planning as a best practice, it's crucial for boards and management to adopt two distinct time perspectives: one dedicated to the long-term development of talent, and the other attentive to the sequencing of critical processes and events leading up to and immediately following the succession date.

## CREATING THE LEADER PROFILE

The continuous availability of strong, deep pools of executive talent within an organization is crucial for a company's long-term stability and growth. Having that bench strength of talent ensures a steady flow of seasoned individuals ready to step into the varied leadership roles within the organization, including that of the CEO. To thoroughly cultivate internal candidates, the best of which will succeed the standing CEO, it's important that boards and management together adopt a long-term frame of reference.

In their partnership with the CEO, the role of the board is to continuously monitor the changing dynamics of the global business environment and that of the company's industry, markets, and competition. In view of this active landscape, the board establishes the strategic direction of the organization and the near-term and long-term leadership talents and skills needed to guide the company into its future. The resulting leadership profile—in essence, a blueprint for the development of all officer positions—becomes a living document reviewed and agreed to annually among board members and between the board and the CEO.

The CEO's role is to use this leadership profile to identify potential succession candidates early on in his or her administration and make certain that the company's talent development program is a purposeful, orchestrated sequence of experiential events that nurtures the growth, development, and retention of each candidate. A five-to-ten-year time frame allows the best talent to develop thoroughly and rise to the top through challenging assignments and fair and objective evaluations.

Internal candidates are typically individuals who reside at company headquarters, such as the CFO, the COO, and the general counsel, and have been in their position for several years, gaining executive-level experience by addressing the issues and decisions expected of an officer of the corporation.

If from this officer pool, the CFO is chosen to be a CEO succession candidate, and that individual has never experienced P&L line responsibility, the company may want that executive to take on a two-to-four-year assignment as head of a business unit. During that period, the controller, or director of finance, or someone from outside the organization will need to assume the role and responsibility of the CFO while the sitting CFO runs a division of the organization.

Additionally, in global companies with operations and markets around the world, it's a standard requirement that candidates live and work in another country in order to appreciate the complexities of working across cultures and to develop an understanding of the business from a global, non-domestic perspective. In order to gain that experience, candidates will need to work "in-country" for at least two to three years in addition to their officer-level position with business unit experience. One can begin to see how the well-rounded development of an internal candidate can easily stretch out over the course of three to ten years.

## SEQUENCING THE SUCCESSION PROCESS

Once the most promising future leaders ascend out of long-term development and are selected as potential successors to the CEO role, orchestrating the leadership succession process, including the final sequencing of assessments, decisions, and assignments, may still take two to three years to complete.

At this near-term stage, in order for directors to make a thoroughly informed selection decision, they must have first-hand knowledge of the talents and skills of the candidates, and not just rely on development reports offered by the CEO.

So that directors may evaluate the business and social intelligence of potential CEO successors, candidates should meet with the board as often as time and situations allows, from in-depth discussions of strategic significance, to informal social events.

While it's important to assess each candidate's business and relational skills, it is equally important for board members and successors to get to know each other over a period of time—preferably two to three years prior to the CEO transition date. With frequency comes familiarity, ultimately giving directors a more accurate picture of the consistency and authenticity of each candidate.

It is important to note here that best practice is to have more than one internal candidate. A recurring theme that emerged during the in-depth interviews we conducted with board chairs and CEOs is that a number of failed successions were the result of boards and management risking everything on one candidate who dropped out within months of the transition date, forcing the board to look outside for a successor at the last minute. Given the psychological and organizational issues mentioned earlier, it's a challenge to have more than one candidate in the running. But these issues must be worked through, for having two or more candidates in the running unquestionably puts the company in the best possible position for the future.

Two to three years prior to the succession date, whether or not the board and CEO conclude that the succession candidates have the necessary talents and skills, it's still considered best practice for the board to engage a search firm to benchmark external talent and evaluate how well their internal candidates match up to the capabilities of outside executives. If the board concludes that its internal candidates don't measure up to the experience and skills of the external talent, there is still adequate time to hire outside talent and see to it that they are sufficiently integrated into the culture and strategy of the company.

Within 9 to 12 months of the CEO transition date, the board should begin to make final assessments of its internal candidates to determine if it indeed has a successor. If so, an internal succession will most likely require the advancement of positions two or three levels deep within the organization. For example, if the CFO is selected to become the CEO, then the company will require a new chief financial officer and controller.

So any of these moves will require interdependent, sequential maneuvers that must be planned out well in advance of the date of transition.

If 9 to 12 months out the board discovers that its internal candidates are not capable of fulfilling the leadership profile, the board has enough time to employ a search firm and conduct a formal external search. This process will require at least this amount of time preceding the transition date to give the search firm enough time to identify available talent, provide the board with options, and for the board to vet final candidates. And if an external successor is offered the position—most likely an existing officer of another company—that candidate will require time to evaluate and negotiate the offer and, if accepting, will have to give at least two months' advance notice before resigning his or her current post.

Once the successor is selected, three to six months prior to the new CEO taking office, the board and company have adequate time to introduce the successor to the business media and various stakeholders. Additionally, a measure often overlooked until the successor actually assumes office is his or her appointment to the board prior to the transition date. This allows the incoming CEO to interact and align with the board, meet key customers, engage the analyst community, shareowners, and other stakeholders, and in the exchange, gain a deeper appreciation for the nuances of governance.

Finally, there should be at least three months of pre-transitioning between the outgoing and incoming CEO. In these strategy sessions, the outgoing CEO can fully transfer his or her knowledge of and insights into the industry to the incoming CEO. Strategic and operational discussions could also include insights into the executive team, markets, key customers, and competitors.

Once the new CEO is in office, it's tempting for the board to breathe a sigh of relief and feel that the transition process is complete. Conversely, our research shows that 41 percent of directors do not believe they pay sufficient attention to the integration of a new CEO and his or her alignment with the board, the strategic heading of the company, the executive team, or key customers.[1] This lack of integration is one of the greatest reasons for short, unsuccessful tenures and the high rate of CEO failures—many within the first year of a new CEO's term.[2]

Additionally, integration is more involved than originally thought, and given the greater complexity of business, takes much longer than the traditional three-month "honeymoon" period usually allowed by most organizations. While the first 100 days are critical, a new CEO's integration does not stop at that point. Current research shows that successful integration actually takes between 12 and 18 months, whether the successor is internal or external to the organization.[3]

## WORKING BACK

For a full perspective of the time sequencing of these stages of development and how far in advance a board should be planning for succession, an approach adopted by many of the boards we've worked with is to begin with the date of CEO transition and then to work back from that date—in essence, developing a reverse timeline. Note that the process begins again with the new CEO identifying and seeing to the development of the next round of succession candidates.

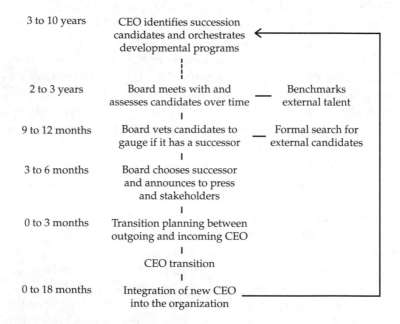

### Working Back
#### From the Date of Transition

| | | |
|---|---|---|
| 3 to 10 years | CEO identifies succession candidates and orchestrates developmental programs | |
| 2 to 3 years | Board meets with and assesses candidates over time | Benchmarks external talent |
| 9 to 12 months | Board vets candidates to gauge if it has a successor | Formal search for external candidates |
| 3 to 6 months | Board chooses successor and announces to press and stakeholders | |
| 0 to 3 months | Transition planning between outgoing and incoming CEO | |
| | CEO transition | |
| 0 to 18 months | Integration of new CEO into the organization | |

Figure 6.1: Working Back From the Date of Transition

## BEING PREPARED

It's uncommon for a CEO to articulate firmly and clearly when he or she is planning to retire, unless there's a high level of trust with the board chair or lead director, as discussed in Chapter 5. It's often a risky move for a CEO to share that kind of information. By disclosing an anticipated departure date, a CEO may feel that he or she is signaling to the board a preoccupation with leaving office, bringing into question the CEO's commitment to the company. It may trigger the board to begin the succession process earlier than the CEO would like. It may also leave the CEO with the impression that he or she can't have a change of heart once they specify a retirement date. For these and many other reasons, CEOs tend to keep their end date to themselves and that's one of the barriers that has to be wrestled with when a board and a CEO sit down to have a conversation about setting succession time frames.

In light of this, what a board can do is develop hypothetical end-date scenarios, and the time continuum above proves very useful in that regard. One begins to see that the early and ongoing development of candidates is the best assurance that a company can be ready in the event of a sudden, unplanned departure or even given a somewhat-planned departure with only one or two years' advance notice.

John Hanson, non-executive chairman and former CEO of Joy Global, reflects on the extensive process he undertook to find his own successor:

> Joy Global is a very complex services business with a significant global manufacturing capability and global service presence. It's a business that has an intense customer contact and focus, and requires a leader with a strong level of technical knowledge and operational knowledge. For this reason, the board and I began to plan my retirement from the CEO post six years before the end of my tenure at 65. It became clear to us that we simply didn't have an internal successor who was capable of stepping into the CEO role in the way we felt was necessary to continue to drive the company forward.
>
> So our succession planning process included recruiting multiple candidates from the outside and having them run individual divisions, to focus their development over the first

couple of years on really learning the business, learning the strategic direction and intent, and establishing themselves as effective leaders at the operating level.

Later in the process, we determined who among those candidates was capable of assuming the role and we began to work out a development process that focused on specific skill sets and exposure in various international settings. Almost two years after that, we took on a much more focused role where the board itself sat down with what we deemed to be the final candidate, and outlined their expectations for his final development and for the specific issues that they believed needed to be addressed for him to successfully serve in that role. That entire process took six years. For a company as global and complex as ours, the CEO succession planning process must always be viewed in the context of a never-ending continuum of talent development.[4]

## Need-Based Versus Time-Based

In addition to not having deep pools of executive talent and well-planned transitions, there is another danger in approaching CEO succession as an episodic event that occurs once every five to ten years—a focus and dependence on tenure versus competence. Business no longer evolves, it transforms, and the talents and skills a CEO brings to the office at the onset of his or her term may no longer be adequate two or three years following.

The key insight here is that directors should be monitoring the changing business landscape and periodically asking themselves if the company has the right leader with the right skills at the right time in order to sustain the success and growth of the organization.

Doing this not only helps candidates in the pipeline to develop future skills to match the company's strategic heading, but also encourages the ongoing development of the incumbent CEO. It's uncommon for CEOs to acknowledge that their talents and skills may no longer address the needs of their changing company, and to accept that it's not about serving out their remaining time in office, but if they should actually continue serving as company leader at all.

# A Noble Decision

William Ford's decision to step aside as CEO of Ford Motor Company in 2006, cutting short his term in office, was considered by industry analysts at the time to be a bold, intelligent, and mature action that was necessary in order to move the company forward. As chairman and CEO, Ford recognized that, given the changing business environment, he was not the best person to run the company and, for that reason, decided not serve out his full term. In a televised press conference several weeks before his self-truncated date of transition, he unveiled his reasons for stepping down as CEO and naming Boeing's Alan Mulally as his successor, admitting, in no uncertain terms, that he was not the person for the job:

> . . . The business model that sustained us for decades is no longer sufficient to sustain profitability. We needed somebody who had extensive turnaround experience, who was a leader, and a real team builder . . . In this environment, with a relatively young management team facing tough times, I felt that we could benefit from the leadership of someone who had been through similar tough times and had led a team through those challenges successfully.[5]

The unplanned succession of William Ford is a classic example of a need-based versus time-based view of leadership. It was William Ford's commitment to saving his company, and in the end, the Ford legacy, that compelled him to step down as CEO and, in doing so, secure a more solid footing for the future of the company. But it was also an impassioned lead director and governance expert, Irvine Hockaday, Jr., along with a board comprised exclusively of former CEOs, who together, in special and highly confidential sessions, hashed out the issues facing Ford as well as the macroeconomic and global forces that were battering the automotive industry.[6]

William Ford showed the depth of his commitment to the company and its legacy when he asked Hockaday to let Mulally know that he would step aside as chairman and offer that title to Alan as well if Alan would accept the position of CEO. It may well have been Ford's selfless offer that cinched the deal in Mulally's mind. It turned out Mulally would accept the Ford CEO position only if the board would guarantee that William Ford would remain on as chairman to provide him the bridge of experience and knowledge of the business.[7]

## BALANCING TIMING AND STAKEHOLDER INTERESTS

A crucial aspect of succession planning is in getting the timing right. Having the chosen candidate ready at the exact time the incumbent leaves office is virtually impossible. The succession planning exercise, however, needs adequate time and pacing so that it is neither too slow or too fast a developmental time frame. Delaying the start of the exercise or phasing it in too slowly might result in internal candidates not having adequate time for personal development and a fair and thorough assessment. Too late a start or not starting at all could result in high-potential candidates underdeveloped and overlooked in favor of an external successor.

Accelerating the succession planning process to ensure that the successor is ready to take over before the incumbent's departure causes problems as well. Candidates, fully developed and ready to lead, may become prospects for recruiters or may decide to leave the company on their own for better prospects.

If a CEO stays on too long, he or she becomes a detriment to the process, as the company may lose a potential successor who might accept an outside offer because it appears the CEO is not considering stepping down. Additionally, successors-in-waiting could create an uneasy and tense situation within their own departments or business units, potentially causing organizational issues as interdependent moves are postponed as the board waits for the CEO's decision to step down. Working back from an agreed-upon end date with the CEO is the only solution to an otherwise untenable planning and talent retention environment.

Douglas Conant, former CEO of Campbell Soup Company, director of Campbell Soup Company, and a trustee of The Conference Board, believes that allowing the board sufficient lead time will more than likely result in a well-informed and well-timed choice. Moreover, candidates who are given adequate time to prove themselves will see the process as fair and companies stand a better chance of retaining the candidates who don't get the top spot.

If I were to pick the one succession process that went best, it would be my Applebee's experience where I was chairman of the compensation committee. Our attentiveness to a timetable that allowed for extensive development and observation of two excellent candidates made all the difference in the world.

Applebee's was a small restaurant concept that became the largest casual dining concept in the world. It exploded with growth. Lloyd Hill was there at the start up and recruited to be Chairman and CEO. Six years into that role, he told the board that he was planning on retiring at 60—literally three to four years before his actual retirement. There were no surprises and everybody on the board felt connected to the process.

The CEO had two internal candidates that he felt were quite strong, and his challenge over the next three to four years was going to be to develop both of them so that the board could make an informed choice, or go outside if the board felt it needed to.

Our early and candid discussions with the incumbent enabled us to orchestrate a thorough development planning agenda with the CEO, creating several opportunities every year for the board to interact with the candidates. We saw them present to the organization, at shareholders meetings, at sales meetings, and at franchisee meetings. We had good visibility into each candidate's performance because the CEO was very committed to each leader's development and he kept the board engaged.

This extensive development process also kept the candidates engaged to the point where they both felt they had a good shot with fair feedback. One was promoted to CEO and the other decided to stay on as CFO. It was such a thoughtful, transparent process with good intentions and high engagement, but most importantly, we had sufficient lead time to allow the board to make a highly informed decision in the end.[8]

## Discussing Timelines with the CEO

The best starting point for working back from a transition date in order to plan, orchestrate, and sequence the thorough cultivation of internal candidates is to secure the end point. But how does a board nail down the CEO on his or her end date? How do directors deal with the natural resistance of a newly minted CEO to contemplate planning their departure at the onset of their tenure?

There are many benefits and experiences that make letting go very difficult. Usually, the compensation of the CEO is higher than that of any other employee in the organization. Similar to compensation are the perks that come with the top position such as a seasoned personal assistant, a company jet, or a suite at the sports arena. Last, but certainly not least, is the incredible status that comes with the position of CEO, for with status comes power. And human nature being what it is, power is the most difficult force to surrender to another. The CEO needs to realize that informing the board six months to a year before retiring is not nearly enough advance notice. It's been proven time and again that gap in leadership can cause the loss of stakeholder trust and confidence, the erosion of share value, and the exodus of future talent.

The key insight is instilling a higher level of awareness in the CEO and re-directing his or her attention away from personal power and personal gain and toward the needs of the organization. In fact, when a new CEO comes on board, a conscientious board chair or independent director should have that candid conversation with the CEO as early as possible in the new leader's term of office so the discussion of an end date is not misinterpreted as a vote of no confidence. The board chair or lead director must stress the importance of succession planning and the realistic time frame required for broad and thorough candidate development, and that an approximate end date is the only way a board can best prepare and begin to work back from that transition date.

Even if the CEO's annual appraisal is strong and the company is posting record profits and increased stock value, a board chair or lead director and the CEO should have a conversation at least once a year confirming the CEO's own plans and intentions. And while the CEO doesn't necessarily have to say, "Well, in three years I plan on stepping down," the board chair or lead director must impart that it's in the best interest of the CEO's legacy and continued success of the company to ensure that there is continuity in leadership.

Stephen Patrick, retired vice chairman of Colgate-Palmolive Company, and current director of Arrow Electronics, believes getting the CEO to buy into the succession planning is a condition of the job, and a transition date should be established and agreed to even before the candidate is hired. This is an excellent, non-threatening way of getting a new CEO engaged from the onset, instead of having a discussion of end dates a year or two into the job when he or she may interpret the conversation as a vote of no confidence.

I believe the existing CEO has to take ownership of the succession plan five years before he's going to step down. I think it takes that long. And if you don't have the CEO involved in the process, you've got a problem.

A new, young CEO will interpret that request as a threat, the idea of looking for someone to replace him. This, I find, is the most challenging aspect of succession planning—getting the incumbent to buy into the process at the onset and own a part of it. They key is to have that understanding before the CEO even gets started—to make that condition part of the interview process.

A board can certainly take charge of the matter, but it's always better to have the CEO partner in the process and develop internal candidates over a period of time and allow the board enough time to assess the candidates. If you're looking at the process three to five years out, you can determine if you have sufficient candidates internally, and if you don't, you have time to go to the outside and bring someone into the organization and develop that person. The alternative, going to outside at the last minute, is very dangerous because you don't know what you're getting until you've got him.

When I think of the risks a company faces, the number one risk is having the wrong person in the top spot, far beyond financial issues or product-tampering issues, or whatever challenges a company may face. Those are all high-risk things that have to be given their own due diligence, but if you put the wrong person in the job, he or she can destroy 50 years of good work by the company and the board—overnight.[9]

## CONCURRENT SUCCESSION DECISIONS

The last key concern in setting succession time frames is this awkward yet classic dynamic: how do you navigate the transition when the former CEO, who may have been an iconic figure and an integral part of the organization, still holds the title as executive chair, has opinions about every decision, and now has to witness someone else dissembling all that he or she built up over the years? There are two schools of thought on this practice, best informed and guided by the culture of the organization:

- Some believe that when the CEO steps down that he or she should not remain on as chairperson. The concern is that having the former CEO stay on as board chair can impede the thoughts and actions of the incoming CEO.
- Others believe mentoring is valuable and the transfer of strategic and organizational knowledge a critical bridge that should be part of the integration of the new CEO.

Moreover, when the CEO is not the board chair, it is best, for the sake of continuity in governance, to not have the CEO and the board chair turn over at the same time. Best practice is to stagger the turnover of the CEO and the chair if possible, or at best, not to let this happen automatically without careful consideration and pre-planning. The board should ask the board committee chartered to oversee succession planning, what the succession plan is for the board chair. The board should also consider the merits of the incumbent CEO serving on the board as a director and mentoring her or his successor. In some instances though, the opposite strategy may be more appropriate. The CEO and chair may have been in close partnership for a number of years and aligned on all business matters. And the board, as part of the succession process, may decide that the corporate strategy requires a new CEO who is able to take the company in a new direction. In this changing environment, it may be discovered that there is a board member who has deep convictions about this new direction and is interested in serving as the board chair. In this instance, it may be wise for the CEO and the board chair to turn over at the same time, wiping the slate clean with a new board chair and a new CEO who together can establish a new partnership and alignment going forward.

## Key Insights

✓ To approach leadership succession planning as a best practice, it's crucial for boards to adopt two time perspectives: the long-term development of candidates and the near-term sequencing of critical processes leading up to and immediately following the transitioning of the CEO.

✓ For a full perspective of the time sequence required for candidate development, and how far in advance a board should be planning for the actual succession, boards should begin with the date of CEO transition and then work back from that date—in essence, developing a reverse timeline.

✓ Boards and CEOs must shift from a time-based to a need-based view of leadership and to recognize that it's not about tenure but competence. Directors should be constantly monitoring the changing business landscape and asking themselves if the company has the right leader with the right skills at the right time in order to sustain the success and growth of the organization.

✓ A board chair or lead director must have a candid conversation with the CEO to stress the importance of succession planning and the realistic time frame required for broad and thorough candidate development, and that an approximate end date is the only way a board can best prepare and begin to work back from that transition date.

✓ Even if the CEO's annual appraisal is strong and the company is posting record profits and increased stock value, a board chair or lead director and the CEO should have a conversation at least once a year confirming the CEO's own retirement plans and intentions.

✓ When the CEO is not the board chair, it's usually good for the sake of continuity in governance to not have both positions turn over at the same time. Best practice is to stagger the turnover, or at best, not to let this happen automatically without giving careful thought to the strategic direction of the company and the merits of having the outgoing CEO serve on the board as mentor to the successor.

# PREPARE FOR EMERGENCIES

# 7

*"Our number one priority has always been our people, and we have some new leaders in key positions—a testament to our deep bench of talent and our commitment to succession planning."*
—James Skinner, former vice
chairman and CEO,
McDonald's Corporation[1]

*"It's been six weeks since the announcement, and the company still hasn't named a replacement. Shareholder groups are saying that it's a sign of weakness and unpreparedness on the part of the board."*
—William Patterson, executive
director, CtW Investment Group[2]

## CALM OR CRISIS?

Shareholders ended up waiting nearly three months for Bank of America's board of directors to name a successor to CEO Ken Lewis, following his surprise resignation announcement on October 1, 2009. You would think the board might have anticipated his departure since shareholders, during a heated annual meeting earlier that April, stripped Lewis of his Chairman's title.[3]

Contrast that with McDonald's naming James Skinner CEO 24 hours after the stepping down of health-stricken Charles Bell, who himself was named CEO the same day James Cantalupo died in office—just six months earlier. These are two very different corporate cultures in their approach to emergency succession planning—one of calm, one of crisis.

Though McDonald's itself experienced an emotional rollercoaster during those two sudden transitions, revenues grew 27 percent while operating income grew 9 percent.[4] The company's employees were aligned in purpose and motivated, and the firm evinced an attitude of calm and stability to its franchise owners, shareowners, customers, and analysts. This was in large part due to the planning and preparedness of its board and management.

In contrast, the board of directors of the largest bank holding company in the United States had no successor in place when Ken Lewis stepped down. Since no internal succession plan was in place, the board had to initiate an outside search and was turned down by more than one executive they pursued. Finally, Brian Moynihan, a talented internal executive, was given the job. The reputation of and trust in Bank of America's board and the company's reputation suffered considerable and sustained damage. And the ripple effect of the board's failure in planning was felt by over 280,000 employees and tens of millions of customers and investors the world over.

## At Its Most Vulnerable

An absence of leadership in today's marketplace—for any period of time—is a very dangerous and risky way to run a business. A company without a leader is left exposed and at its most vulnerable—a situation that can quickly impact employee motivation and productivity, market position, and share value.

The dynamics were quite different a generation ago. Boards were less involved in the succession process, and many CEOs were expected to hand-pick their own successors. Business was more predictable in the 1970s and 80s and so was the succession of leadership. Things have changed in this global age. The pace of business and immediacy of information, accelerating since the late 1990s, now demands a higher level of emergency succession planning. Health issues, an unplanned departure, or a forced resignation or performance-related dismissal of the CEO or other critical members of the executive team are the common circumstances that give rise to an emergency succession event, with an unconditional firing of an officer the highest-risk situation. A sudden departure or removal from office is a telltale sign that the company is either on the brink of a crisis, or well into the chasm of one.

Directors must be ready to contend with an unexpected change of leadership—at any level in the organization and for any reason. They must react quickly, but with calmness and decisiveness. They must assure employees, customers, and investors that new leadership will soon be in place, that the company has a strong footing, that employees are motivated, and that the business will continue to move forward.

## COMPOUNDING THE EMERGENCY

Boards compound emergency succession crises by not being prepared. With backs against the wall and in fear of losing time as they scramble to gain control over an unraveling situation, directors sometimes rush to judgment with tactical rather than strategic, underdeveloped, and unaligned decisions.

The absence of pre-planning significantly increases the likelihood of confusion and uncertainty during an emergency succession, but so do CEOs who assume they know best and use their position of power to exclude their boards from succession discussions and decisions. In the event of the unplanned departure of a CEO, there's a sense of an immediate loss of control on the part of the board, causing the panic that directors feel when blindsided and overwhelmed by an unanticipated succession crisis. It's during these times that boards stand the greatest chance of making its worst decisions, and at the most vulnerable time in a company's history.

## HP's déjà vu

HP's stock price fell 12 percent on the news of Mark Hurd's forced resignation in August 2010, and continued to drop with the growing realization that the largest company in one of the world's fastest-moving industries was operating without a CEO.[5]

HP's board had no formal succession plan in place when it hired Carly Fiorina or Mark Hurd, or even Leo Apotheker, who was parachuted into the position two months after Hurd's departure—and resigned less than a year later. The company's stock dropped 47 percent during Apotheker's 10 months in office.[6]

HP's dismal market performance since 2000—during a decade of remarkable advances and innovations in technology—is due, in large part, to the board's absence of governance in defining a strategic heading for the company and developing and recruiting future leaders along that line.

## ALIGNED ON PURPOSE

A company's vision, as conceived by the board in concert with the CEO, defines the kind of leadership that company will need in order to achieve its short- and long-term objectives. Leaders at all levels are then recruited, developed, and advanced in alignment with that strategic direction.

The organizations that best come to grips with emergency successions rely less on the person at the top than the strategic direction of the company. In the event of a sudden absence of leadership, employees remain focused, motivated, and confident. They know their course of action and know to stay that course.

The key insight is that the departure of any single individual is less of a momentous event when the company is unified in purpose and objective. An unexpected void in leadership is still a critical event and can be undoubtedly be a setback, but it's less of a blow to the system if the organization has a strategic heading and the entire company is actively engaged in running the business. In essence, the purpose of the company survives its leadership.

Skinner was the last surviving author of McDonald's "Plan to Win," a turnaround program initiated in 2003 when he was then vice chairman. "Plan to Win" was the mantra for McDonald's global market strategy and Skinner, assuming the office of CEO, ensured that the company would maintain that global strategy. This was critical to the peace of mind of franchise owners and the trust of employees and investors.[7] The concept of a strategic plan defining the selection of, guiding the tenure of, and surviving the unexpected departure of a CEO is a best practice in companies such as McDonald's, IBM, Johnson & Johnson, GE, Campbell Soup, and McCormick & Company.

Alan Wilson, chairman and CEO of McCormick and board director of the Grocery Manufacturers Association, considers McCormick's emergency succession plan as more of a high-level organizational plan so that, in the event of a sudden change of leadership, McCormick would be able to sustain its solid business footing. By having an emergency succession plan in place, McCormick's intention is to always be ready to bring in a strong internal candidate and never feel pressured to hire an outsider who may result in a cultural or strategic mismatch.

> It's not just the name of a successor in a sealed envelope, but more of a road map for how we organize the company a few levels deep in the event of an unplanned death, departure, or dismissal.
>
> We went through our talent succession discussion with the governance committee and then the full board, to develop a fairly comprehensive emergency plan that, in addition to a series of interrelated successions, also includes things like actual drafted press releases and with whom to communicate, and when and how. We review the emergency plan every year to confirm or make any necessary updates to successors. Having everything defined is more than helpful in the event of an emergency, because people will be operating under pretty extreme duress.
>
> Companies that were paying attention learned a lot from what happened with McDonald's a few years ago. The board got a lot of credit for executing the succession plan, immediately issuing press releases, and dealing with it very effectively. When a company responds in that way, it sends the message to investors that you've been really diligent, and it increases market confidence in the board, in the company, and for the incoming CEO.
>
> Alternatively, the unplanned and poorly managed transitions can have a very negative impact on a company's stock prices and brand. We see it happen year after year. Those are the companies and boards that aren't paying attention.[8]

## A Name Is Not a Plan

Many boards believe they are prepared for an emergency succession because they have the name of a successor in a sealed envelope, ready to be opened at the moment of crisis. What if the heir apparent was chosen merely by right of succession, or confirmed years ago by the prior board or past CEO, and the decision was never revisited? What if the successor is grappling with a change of heart to a work-life issue? What if the candidate has been secretly recruited over the past three to twelve months and is contemplating taking the better offer and giving the board no more than two months' notice?

If all the board has is a name, then that name needs to be reality checked at least annually, or any time a key change is made to the organization's strategy, structure, or leadership. But a name in itself is not a plan. An emergency succession plan requires the coordination of communications, interim leadership staffing, decision making, and a host of activities both inside and outside the firm. There are interrelated moves within the organization that also must be thought through and updated on an ongoing basis. Key players are constantly moving up, laterally, or out as a result of performance and opportunity. Moreover, organizational structures change to address dynamically changing markets, giving rise to the opportunity to develop and assess candidates, or to acquire and evaluate new talent.

## Strategic Development Culture

For decades, General Electric has made leadership succession the top priority of its strategic business planning process, a model for how strategy should define the talents and skills a future leader at GE must possess. GE's succession program generated several candidates to succeed CEO Jack Welch at his retirement in 2001, each observed over a period of years while being rotated through various business assignments. When it came time to choose Welch's successor, the board made its decision in two weeks. If something unfortunate should have happened to Welch at any time during his tenure, the board would have had a wealth of candidates from which to select a more-than-adequate replacement.[9]

The leadership profile needed to deliver the strategic plan should be the blueprint defining the talent and skill requirements of every leader throughout the organization. A company in best practice has a strategic development culture—a culture of internal succession—led by its board of directors, in partnership with the CEO. As a result, board and management are aligned on the strategic direction of the organization, and in agreement on the talents and skills required to lead and succeed on that bearing. Those talents and skills are then honed and tested through the company's leadership development and succession program, visibly supported and driven by the CEO.

Best practice also involves the board periodically meeting with each potential successor over a period of time to become familiar with each candidate's character, business and financial acumen, and social intelligence. When and if the time comes for the board to make an emergency succession decision, it will have a known successor, prepared to step in and lead.

## WORKING THROUGH THE EMERGENCY

During an emergency succession, directors are pressured to make many quick decisions, some of utmost importance to the future of the organization. If there is any confusion as to who is in charge, even if only in the interim, or if there's any uncertainty as what the focus of the organization will continue to be, the effect on employee morale and the market value of the company can be devastating. Bank of America and HP again come to mind.

An emergency succession plan, updated and rehearsed at least once a year, can help boards and management minimize the chaos and risks associated with leadership change. In times of crisis, people don't think as clearly, and relying on quick decision making—especially at the most critical moment in a company's history—increases the likelihood of tactical errors or oversights. The best organizations are prepared and practiced with an emergency succession plan that consists of defined roles, tested scenarios, and emergency organization and communication programs that the board and management can execute at a moment's notice.

## Crisis Strikes!

In the event of the sudden departure of a CEO, the best of all circumstances is to have a capable and proven successor ready to step in and move the company forward. An interrelated series of officer and executive successions will most likely also take place, almost simultaneously, with capable leadership stepping in to each position. A company spokesperson delivers a calm and confident message to employees, key constituents, investors, and the public that "things are well in hand," heading off potential damage to the company and reputation of the board, and protecting the interests of shareholders. The board and company appear as a genuinely unified team to employees, customers, and investors alike.

If no successor is ready to step in, or the "ready" successor cannot serve for some reason, the board selects the interim leader from a short list of internal candidates confirmed just months ago. The spokesperson conveys the same message that the company is maintaining its heading, is confident in its interim CEO, and will soon name a successor. In the background, there are different emergency procedures underway—scenarios already thought through as internal candidates undergo final assessments or the board approves a formal external search among the talent it's been benchmarking for over a year.

## Communicating Calm and Confidence

In the event of a sudden loss of leadership, it's important to determine, up front, who the spokesperson will be—the face of the company to both internal and external audiences. That person will be the one voice to the media, the one in charge, authorized to make corporate-level decisions during the CEO's absence. He or she will serve as the principal point of contact with the board and the senior management team and maintain regular communications with the directors.

One of the most important elements of an emergency succession plan is the communication plan, including draft communications to key customers, business partners, the analyst community, and the media. Best practice is having prepared communications that are updated at least twice a year. Although the draft documents will still have to be filled in with names, dates, and events when the crisis strikes, the basic structure of each communiqué, from its opening core message to the paragraphs containing the company's sentiments, thoughtful biographies of leaders, mission focus of the company, etc., are written in advance. This may not seem as an important enough element for which to pre-plan, but at the onset of an emergency, there is the human tendency to freeze, or overreact, or improperly assume control. A sound communication plan will send a powerful message of calm and confidence to all constituencies.

Communications to employees, customers, and investors, in words and actions, must convey that the company has an emergency succession plan underway, that there is strong organizational morale and motivation, that the company is maintaining its business heading, and that the board will be ready to name the successor shortly.

## Minimizing the Causes

At the beginning of this chapter, we spoke of how boards exacerbate emergencies by not being prepared to act in the event of a sudden change in leadership. Out of fear of a loss of momentum, investor confidence, and share value, unprepared boards will often make emotional and tactical mistakes. Being prepared for an emergency is one thing, minimizing or even eliminating the cause for emergencies is quite another. Being aware of health issues, better vetting of successors, and maintaining a trusting, confiding partnership with the CEO all help minimize the possibility of an emergency succession.

## Disclosing Health-Related Issues

A relatively small percentage of emergency CEO turnovers are due to deteriorating health or a death in office. Health-related reasons are always the most traumatic and unexpected. The greater issue is the CEO's willingness to disclose his or her health status to the board, and the board's obligation to share that information with employees, shareholders, customers, and other stakeholders.

From a legal standpoint, the company has a duty to disclose material information that an investor would need to know in order to make an informed decision about whether to buy or sell that company's stock. The difficulty for the board and CEO is determining exactly what and when health information becomes material.

The difficulty of this issue is best illustrated at Apple where CEO Steve Jobs, and the Apple board, faced numerous questions regarding Jobs' health—from the moment he was first diagnosed with pancreatic cancer in October 2003 to the months preceding his death in October 2011.[10]

In 2003, no public announcement was made of Jobs' diagnosis, although the board was made aware of his condition. The issue of Jobs' health resurfaced again in June 2008, when he appeared noticeably thin at a public appearance. Apple CFO Peter Oppenheimer declined to elaborate, stating simply that, "Steve's health is a private matter." Six months later, in January 2009, Apple released a letter from Jobs in which he explained that his recent weight loss was due to a "hormone imbalance." Immediately following this announcement, Apple stock fell 17 percent.

Jobs returned to work in June of 2009, although two weeks prior to his return news leaked that Jobs had received a liver transplant in April. In January 2011, Jobs took a third and final leave of absence, and in an email to employees, explained that he would "continue as CEO and be involved in major strategic decisions." When asked for additional comment, an Apple spokeswoman replied, "We've said all we're going to say."

Experts fall on both sides of the argument on the appropriateness of Apple's disclosure of Steve Jobs' health issues. Throughout this process, the law was on the side of the Apple for not disclosing any more information than it had shared over the course of the past seven years. Attorneys outside the company advised Apple's board that personal privacy trumped disclosure obligations so long as Jobs was able to continue to perform his duties. Even the SEC opened inquiries into the matter in 2006 and 2009, both of which were closed without action.

From an ethical standpoint, though, the answer becomes a little clearer. A CEO has a right to keep details regarding his or her health problems a private matter. But a company officer's right to privacy is not necessarily absolute. In health-related issues, a CEO's privacy rights has to be balanced against the legal obligations the CEO, officers, and board of directors have to their shareholders, employees, and customers.

## Better Upfront Vetting

Forced resignations or unconditional, performance-related dismissals make up a small percentage of emergency CEO turnovers, but these crises have the most devastating effect on employee morale and motivation as well as on the company's market position and stock value.

Unprepared boards, inundated with the pressures of an unplanned CEO turnover, may also be unfamiliar with or lacking confidence in the company's internal talent. In these moments, directors will opt to bring in a quickly vetted outsider, increasing the chance of yet another CEO turnover. During the period 2000 to 2010, external hires resulted in almost twice the CEO failure rate when compared to inside successors.[11]

Boards can nearly eliminate the probability of performance-related dismissals by having in place an internal leadership development and succession program that builds talented, culturally, and strategically aligned candidates. Additionally, boards should look externally to benchmark best practices and best practitioners, so that in the event of an emergency succession with no viable internal candidates ready yet for leadership, a formal search can be conducted among known external talent.

Ford Motor Company's board looked internally, well in advance of William Ford's termination date as CEO, and determined that they didn't have the person to run the company given all the changes buffeting the automotive industry over the past several years. The board had sufficient time to evaluate its short list of external talent and made an offer to Alan Mulally, who accepted, and lead the re-emergence and profitability of Ford.

## Discussing the Future

In Chapter 5, we talked about the role of a lead director and the model of success when a CEO can openly share expectations, concerns, and even fears with a lead director, and trust that he or she is entering into a confiding, fair, and empathetic partnership.

We also described the social intelligence skills of a lead director, which are most beneficial in times of crisis. A perceptive individual with strong relational skills can be a calming force during a difficult stage in the career of a CEO, who may be deliberating over change or conflict in his or her personal life, or contemplating another industry or another career.

An attentive lead director closely studies the psychology of the CEO, to read when he or she is disappointed or disengaged. There may be family issues or personal issues, forcing the sitting CEO to change perspectives on his or her future. Recruiters can draw away talented CEOs with new and exciting challenges, higher compensation, and greater benefits. Recruiters can also draw away talent one to two levels below the CEO, requiring emergency succession preparedness at all levels of leadership. Was Boeing ready to replace Alan Mulally, president and CEO of Boeing Commercial Airplanes, when Ford's board of directors offered him the CEO position?

The key insight is not just being prepared for emergency succession, but in significantly reducing or even eliminating the causes of such emergencies. Have a strategic plan that defines the leader profile and guides the company's leadership development and succession program. Have candidates in job rotations to ensure a continuous resource of high-integrity leadership ready to step in tomorrow or in two years—what McDonald's calls its "one ready now, one ready future" succession plan.[12]

Realize that continuous leadership development and time-tested assessment of candidates by the board can significantly reduce if not eliminate the possibility of the forced resignation or dismissal of a CEO.

Finally, the board and CEO should review the emergency succession plan at least annually. They should scenario-plan the potential loss of leadership in key areas of the business and ensure candidates are in development for each critical position. Annual discussions must take place between the chair or lead director and CEO to know what is on the CEO's mind and confirm his or her plans for the foreseeable future.

# Key Insight

✓ Boards compound emergency succession crises by not being prepared for an unexpected change of leadership. With backs against the wall and in fear of losing time as they scramble to gain control over an unraveling CEO succession crisis, directors will often rush to judgment with tactical, under-developed, and unaligned decisions.

✓ The organizations that endure emergency successions the best are the ones that are less person-dependent and more reliant on the strategic direction of the company. The key insight is that the departure of any single individual is less of a momentous event when the company and its employees are unified in purpose and objectives.

✓ Many boards believe they are prepared for an emergency succession because they have a name in a sealed envelope—but a name is not a plan. An emergency succession plan requires the coordination of communications, interrelated moves within the organization, interim leadership for time-sensitive issues, and a host of ancillary activities that must be updated and scenario-planned at least annually.

✓ One of the most important elements is the communication plan, including draft communications to key customers, business partners, the analyst community, and the media. Clear communication with the right tone can send a powerful message of calm and confidence to all constituencies.

✓ A company in best practice has a strategic development culture, a culture of internal succession, led by its board of directors in partnership with the CEO. As a result, board and management are aligned on the strategic direction of the organization and in agreement on the talents and skills required to lead and succeed on that bearing.

✓ The key insight is not just being prepared for emergency successions but significantly reducing or even eliminating the causes. Review emergency plans at least annually. Scenario-play loss of leadership in key areas and ensure candidates are in ready development. Hold annual discussions with the CEO to confirm his or her plans for the next few years. Know what is on the CEO's mind.

# Align on Strategy and Profile

## 8

*"It may be important to achieve collegiality on a board, but what's more important is authenticity. If constructive debates and even arguments are needed to reach alignment on strategy and leadership requirements, then so be it! For if either are lacking, then success will be severely compromised."*

—Daniel W. Duval, former
chairman and
independent lead director,
Arrow Electronics, Inc.

By including *Align on Strategy and Profile* as one of the 10 Key Dimensions to effective CEO succession planning, our intent is to characterize why boards and management, actively involved and strategically aligned on the future direction of the company, are so essential to sustained organizational performance and effective CEO succession planning. When approached with candor and genuine consensus, a company's board of directors and CEO can, together, advance a well-reasoned strategic vision and plan for the company, determine the talents and skills required of the CEO to achieve that plan, and provide management a blueprint for the development of the organization's future leaders along that strategic heading.

## IN THE ABSENCE OF STRATEGY

CEO succession is a milestone event that can either reinforce or alter the course of a company's strategic heading. When there is change at the top, the organization's vision, values, culture, strategy, and market value should all be revisited. A well-strategized CEO succession plan can minimize turmoil, initiate purposeful change, and create opportunities for innovation and growth. Without thorough planning, the disruption caused by a change in CEOs can defocus and derail an organization.

We have all witnessed companies—increasingly in the past 20 years—who have lost their competitive edge and stalled forward momentum due to a poorly planned CEO succession that put the wrong leader in the top position. The business world is peppered with examples of companies that became their own worst enemies because of an absence of deep strategic thinking at the board level, lack of consensus on the future of the company, and as a result, failure to select the right CEO to lead the business forward.

## No Previous Experience Required

In September 2011, Yahoo! Inc. fired its CEO Carol Bartz, after more than two-and-a-half years of dismal market performance and stagnant share value. Bartz was Yahoo!'s third CEO in a little over four years, widening the gap in the heated Internet advertising race to online search leaders Google and Facebook.[1] Bartz arrived at Yahoo! as a respected Silicon Valley executive who had won praise for turning around business software maker Autodesk Inc., but she had no previous experience in Internet advertising, Yahoo!'s primary source of revenue. Although talented in her own right, that critical void on her resume immediately raised questions whether she was qualified for the top job at Yahoo!, and those doubts by investors and analysts only escalated as Yahoo!'s revenue spiraled downward during her short term of office.

The disappointing performance was reflected in Yahoo!'s stock price at her departure, which closed only 7 percent higher than when Bartz was hired as CEO. During the same period, Google's stock price grew by more than 66 percent.[2]

In the face of the company's struggling advertising business, high attrition rate of talented engineers, and stagnant product innovation cycle, Yahoo!'s future seems unclear. And while the board is embarking on a strategic review to determine the company's future, it has, at the same time, engaged a search firm to find its fourth CEO since 2009—without first deciding on a strategic corporate vision and the necessary skills and experiences of the next leader.

## An Uncertain Future

After just 10 months on the job, HP forced the resignation of Leo Apotheker, the most recent setback for a company that's been besieged by a decade of disagreement at the board level and abrupt CEO departures (three in six years)—a company now considered by many investors, customers, and analysts to be in strategic drift.

Former head of European software giant SAP, Apotheker, who was let go by SAP just a year earlier, was considered a questionable choice by many analysts to lead HP—since it's predominantly a hardware company. Most of HP's directors didn't even meet Apotheker before hiring him.[3]

The plunge in the company's stock value came when Apotheker announced HP would spin off its PC division, exit the mobile device business that it had just entered with a $1.2 billion purchase of Palm in 2010, and spend $10.5 billion to buy U.K. software producer Autonomy. With Apotheker's overhaul of the HP board, naming six new members during the course of his short term in office, it's unclear whether the company will be able to reverse some of Apotheker's strategic decisions.[4]

Former eBay CEO Meg Whitman, Apotheker's successor, had been on HP's board for eight months prior to accepting the role of CEO. Whitman, whose clear strengths are in consumer retail, will be challenged to regain the confidence of HP's corporate enterprise customers and be a driver for HP as it changes its strategic heading now toward software and services and away from its core hardware business.

## FROM COMPLACENCE TO CONSENSUS

Defining the strategic direction of the company and the leadership skills required to advance the organization into that future are arguably the most fundamental responsibilities of a board. The board's approval of these two linked decisions ultimately determines the future direction of the company and the most capable leader to devise the strategies that will grow and sustain the organization.

But as we discovered in other areas of responsibility and best practice by boards, knowing is one thing, accomplishing the task is quite another. In our experience, directors clearly understand their legal and fiduciary responsibility to govern and build the company's resources and lay the foundation for its future. Their challenge, though, is not in acknowledging and accepting that responsibility, but in setting aside their differences, conquering their apprehensions, working through personality conflicts, and coming together as one for the benefit of the organization. The devil here is not in the theory of what is best practice but in the execution of it.

Psychological factors and organizational dynamics surrounding the strategic planning process can undermine open and honest discussion and collaboration. And board members' passivity in the presence of strong personalities, self-serving alliances, or cliques among old and new board members, can inhibit the sharing of visions and ideas, suppress critical discussions on business strategy, and cause the board to inadequately define the skills and capabilities required of the CEO.

The key insight here is that, even in the face of these interpersonal challenges, every board member must make every effort to approach the strategic planning process with the utmost resolve and personal authenticity. The design is for each director to be genuinely involved—not to feign consensus out of a sense of allegiance to a mentor, over-sensitivity to one's perception of recessive status on the board, preoccupation with job security, or fear of appearing inexperienced.

There is also at the heart of this an implicit social contract among board members to be accommodating and collegial, and rocking the boat by challenging or questioning the chair or CEO's vision or strategic decisions could be perceived as showing non-conforming, non-collegial—and in the extreme sense—obstructive behavior. The reality is that conformity without truthfulness can lead to far more complicated and costly issues later. And although collegiality is important, honesty and openness is, in the end, the more principled way to achieving universal and genuine consensus.

Directors must overcome their apprehensions and anxieties, and instead, reflect deeply on the strategic direction of the company. If necessary, they should ask the seemingly unintelligent but direct questions and strive for an honest consensus, even in the face of strong differences of opinion among individual members. To achieve this requires the courage to confront and debate strategic differences in an open and constructive manner.

At the onset of the financial crisis and global recession of 2008, a board director of a Texas regional bank had what his colleagues considered the audacity to question the risk exposure of the bank's acceptance of and participation in credit derivative swaps, collateral debt obligations, and mortgage back securities. Despite concerns about the potential to be derided for asking what might be considered naïve questions, the director's insistence on answers regarding acceptable levels of risk revealed previously unexplored liabilities in the financial instruments, which ultimately led the board to exit the investment strategy altogether, saving the bank from nearly certain bankruptcy.

## CONTINUOUSLY ALIGNED WITH MANAGEMENT

The reasons for many of the short and unsuccessful tenures of new CEOs are usually much more complex than what we can gather in the business press. What we can discern, though, is that irreconcilable differences between boards and recent successors most often result from of a lack of deep strategic reflection and genuine consensus at the board level. More often than not, this leads to selecting the wrong leader for the wrong reasons—such as for general industry knowledge, availability, or celebrity, or for a limited set of reasons, such as for negotiating a significant acquisition or implementing cost-cutting measures. Thoughtful strategic planning and real consensus as a basis for effective CEO succession planning helps boards develop and select the right candidate with the right set skills.

Alternatively, strategically aligning with an incumbent CEO carries with it a unique set of interpersonal challenges. Given the pace of change and disruption in business today, a company's strategic heading can reach a crossroads midway through a sitting CEO's term of office. And a board and CEO may find that their vision for the future of the company has diverged, influenced by new technologies, new competition, emerging markets, or changing consumer interests.

The sitting CEO may have been the right leader at the right time, but times change, and even the brightest and most capable leaders may find it difficult to keep pace, or market forces may shift in a direction outside of the incumbent's core competencies. Throughout the CEO's tenure, the board and CEO must strive to maintain strategic alignment, not just on the business-at-hand, but also on the future direction of the company. While the board must be the ultimate body that endorses the company's business strategy, it is best developed through a partnership between the board and the incumbent CEO and reviewed at least annually.

Unexplored and unresolved disconnects between directors and incumbent CEOs brought on by the same psychological forces that can disrupt consensus building among board members can eventually lead to divisiveness between boards and their CEOs. This can result in lost business opportunities, stalled momentum, and resignations or even terminations of once-successful CEOs.

## Differing Visions of the Future

Advanced Micro Devices stock fell 7.6 percent as investors speculated on the reasons for CEO Dirk Meyer's departure announcement in January 2011.

Industry analysts believed the underlying reason was the AMD board's disagreement with Meyer on the company's strategic direction. The board wanted to increase the company's market growth in smartphones, tablets, and mobile devices while Meyer's desire was to maintain AMD's focus on making microchips for personal computers and servers—to step up its competition against Intel and improve its number two position in that market.[5]

Meyer had been with AMD since 1995, holding a variety of prominent engineering roles before becoming the highly regarded successor to CEO Hector Ruiz, which occurred in July 2008. During Meyer's short tenure as CEO, AMD's share grew 60 percent as the company regained its financial footing. Under Meyer, the company developed new products, including the new Fusion line of combination graphics and processor chips. In 2009, he oversaw the final steps of the spinoff of AMD's manufacturing operations into a separate company, Global Foundries, relieving AMD of the huge expense of running chip plants, and allowing it to focus on the higher-margin design business.

Although successful in succession and successful in growing the company during his tenure, Meyer's focus for growth fell out of alignment with the board's vision for the future of AMD.

After eight months of unsuccessfully searching for Meyer's replacement, AMD's board hired Rory Read in August 2011. Read, former COO of Lenovo and specializing in turnarounds, was selected for his turnaround expertise and has been asked to develop a cohesive vision for the company's new strategic direction and then structure the company and its initiatives around it.[6]

## Agree to Disagree

In March 2011, Gianfranco Lanci, CEO of the Taiwanese computer maker Acer, resigned following disagreements with the board over the future direction of the world's third-largest computer maker. Lanci came to Acer from Texas Instruments when Acer bought the TravelMate laptop PC business from TI in 1997, was named president of Acer in 2005, and CEO in 2008.[7]

The company's laptop business had been the source of double-digit growth at the company for years, and helped catapult Acer into the top three in the global PC industry behind HP and in constant competition with Dell for the second ranking. Acer rode higher in 2008 and 2009 on the popularity of its netbooks, inexpensive mini-laptops that fit well in the company's strengths as a maker of low-priced consumer PCs.

The netbook market sharply declined in 2010 with Apple's introduction of the iPad tablet, which immediately led to a wave of competing tablets and other mobile Internet devices from other vendors, all of which eroded Acer's netbook sales. Lanci and a majority of the board held different views on the company's future and could not reach consensus on Acer's strategic direction. Lanci wanted to build on Acer's leadership in the PC market while the board saw a greater need to change the company's business strategy to keep pace with changes in technology, and gain a greater share of the mobile Internet device market.[8] Given the speed of change in business today, differences are expected to occur among board members and between boards and their CEOs. At times, these differences are unsolvable and parting ways may be the only solution. But with open and genuine communication, the differences can be revealed early on, discussed, and potentially resolved, and an unplanned, disruptive transition at the top minimized or even avoided.

The responsibility of the board in the strategic planning process is to make every effort to work in concert with the CEO. This is at the very core of effective board governance. The changing business environment requires constant recalibration of the business strategy and directors along with the CEO must willingly approach this strategic challenge in a close and genuine partnership. The upsides are continuity of leadership, strong employee morale, retention of executive talent, and sustained momentum. The downsides to avoiding this issue are always disruptive and, in the long-run, far worse than the temporary challenges found in navigating difficult and emotionally charged conversations, for the CEO may not be the only loss to the company in the end.

## THE CRITICAL ROLE OF THE LEAD DIRECTOR—FACILITATING CONSENSUS

Over the years, we've discovered that a key factor in successful succession planning is a non-executive chair or lead director who personally orchestrates the way in which board ownership of the succession planning process is defined and managed in partnership with the CEO.

Dealing with a board that is pressing to move forward with succession planning is most often a wrenching, unwanted reality for a CEO. It takes a perceptive individual with strong relational skills to be a calming force during this difficult chapter in the career of a CEO and to lessen that CEO's fears of being overpowered by the board's necessary advancement of the succession process.

The same facilitative dynamic can benefit the strategic planning process between the board and the CEO. An attentive lead director can be very instrumental in navigating the discussions and decisions involving the strategic future of the company and the leadership requirements of the successor CEO. The lead director can also be helpful in tactfully informing an incumbent CEO that his or her skills and capabilities may need updating.

It's very likely that a CEO, who isn't planning to retire for another five to seven years, may require expanded or updated skills in order to continue to move the company forward throughout his or her term of office, whether to stay abreast of new technologies, preside over new acquisitions, or enter new markets.

The key insight here is that at the heart of this convergence between the board and the CEO is a non-executive chair or lead director with the emotional intelligence and endurance to facilitate the strategic planning process. It's a model for success when the board and CEO can openly express what may be very divergent visions for the future of the company, and in the end, genuinely agree on a well-developed strategic direction.

## ALIGNED ON THE LEADER PROFILE

In developing the strategic plan, the board and CEO not only establish the strategic direction of the organization, but also define the near- and long-term leadership talents and skills needed to guide the company into that future. That resulting Leader Profile—in essence, the CEO position profile and blueprint for the development of the company's key talent—becomes a living document, reviewed and recalibrated at least annually to reflect any changes made to the strategic plan, and approved by board members and management.

Just as egos, political issues, and competing agendas affect decisions regarding the strategic direction of the organization, so too can these challenges impede or derail the board's decisions regarding CEO succession. When boards review their CEO succession plans, individual directors often approach the discussions with a candidate in mind and their thoughts and comments on the leadership requirements of the next CEO can be influenced by the characteristics of their preferred nominee. Such competing agendas have the potential to compromise strategic plans and scuttle leadership development programs. This invariably results in hastily chosen successors with short, unsuccessful tenures, regardless of how structured and detailed a board's succession planning program may have been.

Having the strategic plan define the leader profile is the best method for offsetting the "personal favorites" approach to candidate selection. By allowing the strategic plan to define the skills and traits required of the succeeding CEO, boards can sidestep the power plays and personality issues that frequently arise during CEO succession planning. The key insight here is for board members to maintain their objectivity and to hold off deciding on and promoting their preferred candidates too early in the process.

Boards should remain attentive to the continuous development of the company's top leadership, ensuring that the skills and abilities of the organization's executive team are aligned to the strategic plan. To that end, the leader profile is also a useful guide for the ongoing development and appraisal of the incumbent CEO.

Peter Fasolo, chief human resource officer at Johnson & Johnson and former chief talent officer at Kohlberg Kravis Roberts & Company (KKR), recalls his experience in using the strategic plan as a guiding template for defining the skills and capabilities of the CEO and other company officers across KKR's portfolio of companies.

> One of our portfolio companies had a need for a CEO as the sitting CEO was transitioned out and the board put in place a very capable interim CEO, giving the board time to go out to the marketplace and benchmark external talent. We actively engaged with the board on a broader context or set of conditions in looking for this talent so it wasn't just "here are the specs of the job and go out and look." It was more, "let's first take a look at the strategy of the company over the next five years, and find someone who has the necessary talents and skills to lead this company into the future."
>
> We stepped back and really had a robust conversation with the board around industry dynamics, where are things going domestically and globally, what are the competitive threats that are likely to loom on the horizon, what's the history of the firm, where have they been successful, and where have they miss-stepped and why?
>
> We spent a lot of time strategizing with the board in order to understand the dynamics that were taking place in the company

today, in the current operational challenges that were unique to this company, and in the dynamics that were likely to take place over the next five years. Placing the CEO or any officer in a role is not just about what talents and skills are required today, but what will be required for the future.[9]

The leader profile also becomes a valuable tool for benchmarking external talent while, at the same time, developing a company's CEO successor candidates. We'll dig into this process more in Chapter 9.

## GETTING FROM HERE TO THERE— THE CULTURE IMPERATIVE

A well-conceived strategic plan, initiated at the board level through a genuine consensus of all of its directors and in alliance with the CEO, identifies the company's current market position as well as its aspirations for the future. The strategic plan defines how the organization needs to adapt and what resources it needs to develop in order to compete in the global marketplace today and tomorrow. But the strategic plan and the strategic planning process cannot end there, otherwise the exercise results in nothing more than a static plan on paper.

The CEO and senior management must dynamically build out the organization's capabilities to the specifications of the strategic plan, closing the gap between the company's current reality and its desired future outcomes. Even then, the vision for the company is only as good as the talent within it to lead the organization forward.

One of the most critical challenges facing companies today is preparing a new generation of leaders who will extend the strategic reach of their organizations. The most successful companies are the ones that are in constant strategic renewal and alignment. They also happen to be the organizations that maintain highly effective CEO succession planning programs and sustain cultures that succeed at retaining valuable talent. In Chapter 9, we will discuss the value to succession planning in building and maintaining a talent pipeline, but moreover, what companies must do to create a pipeline of future leaders with more than just transactional skills.

## Key Insights

✓ Psychological factors and organizational dynamics surrounding the strategic planning process can undermine open and honest discussion and collaboration. In the face of these challenges, each board member must make every effort to approach the strategic planning process with the utmost resolve and personal authenticity.

✓ The responsibility of the board in the strategic planning process is to make every effort to work in concert with the CEO. This is at the very core of effective board governance. The changing business environment requires constant calibration of the business strategy and directors along with the CEO must willingly approach this strategic challenge in a close and genuine partnership.

✓ At the heart of this convergence between the board and the CEO is a non-executive chair or lead director with the emotional intelligence and endurance to facilitate the strategic planning process. It's a model for success when the board and CEO can openly express what may be very divergent visions for the future, and in the end, genuinely agree on a well-developed strategic heading.

✓ In developing the strategic plan, the board and CEO not only establish the strategic direction of the organization, but also define the near- and long-term leadership talents and skills needed to guide the company into that future. That resulting Leader Profile becomes a living document, reviewed at least annually to reflect any changes made to the strategic plan.

✓ Having the strategic plan define the leader profile is the best method for offsetting the "personal favorites" approach to candidate selection. The key insight here is for board members to maintain their objectivity and to hold off deciding on and promoting their preferred candidates too early in the process.

# BUILD THE TALENT PIPELINE

## 9

*"The ultimate measure of a man is not where he stands in moments of comfort and convenience, but where he stands at times of challenge and controversy."*

—Dr. Martin Luther King, Jr.[1]

Defining the strategic direction of a company and the talents and skills required of its leadership to advance the organization into its future are fundamental responsibilities of a board of directors. The most successful companies are the ones in which board and management approach those responsibilities in close partnership and with genuine consensus. In their alliance, directors and senior management—together—determine what constitutes success and gain a clear understanding of the performance requirements of its company's leadership to achieve that success. Equipped with that insight, executives can leverage the right experiences over the course of their careers and identify the performance behaviors and relationships necessary for their ongoing development.

Companies that build their talent pipelines with such planning discipline produce management cultures that attract and retain the best talent, and they accelerate the development of each generation of leaders with the critical skills needed to sustain corporate growth.

Depending on the industry and the company's strategic plans, those critical skills could include expertise in science, manufacturing or engineering, financial acumen, product and brand development, mergers and acquisitions, restructuring, or managing a global network of independent franchises.

In addition to performance-specific attributes, there are also the demonstrable characteristics most sought after in capable leaders. In a recent global survey of 1,140 companies in 89 countries, the top five traits companies state they most value in their CEOs include strategic thinking, execution, decision making, technical competence, and teamwork.[2]

Nevertheless, what we have learned over the years is that, although vitally important, there is far more to leadership development and succession planning than developing or recruiting CEOs with tangible, measurable skills and overtly visible traits. In working with boards and management, we have often noticed a dimension of leadership missing in many talent development programs and absent from the inventory of skills and traits found in the CEO position profiles used by search firms.

We believe this missing dimension of leadership is what ultimately causes such a high percentage of CEOs to fail early in their tenures— failures rarely attributed to a lack of experience, lack of business knowledge, or lack of competence.

## It's More than Talent

More often than not, CEO failure occurs as a result of poor judgment, a failure to execute, indecisiveness, or personality flaws such as arrogance, self-indulgence, inflexibility, or a command-and-control style of leadership that fails to engender employee trust and inspiration.

In the study cited above, the 1,140 companies that chose those five demonstrable traits as the most critical characteristics needed in today's CEOs were less interested in the attributes of inspiring leadership, influence, emotional intelligence, creativity, resilience, and capacity to learn. Those traits were much further down the list of valued characteristics. These softer characteristics of leadership are less quantifiable, take longer to observe and distinguish, and as a result, are often overlooked by boards and management—often to the detriment of their companies.

Phil Condit, who joined Boeing in 1965 and became CEO and chairman in 1996, was considered by many a visionary engineer whose elegant solutions to aircraft design problems were his greatest contributions to aeronautics. As an engineer, he was considered a brilliant problem solver, though many considered him an indecisive and self-indulgent leader who often seemed aloof and isolated. Conduit resigned as Boeing's CEO in December 2003—a sudden move brought on by defense contracting scandals that ultimately sent two Boeing executives to jail the following year. Condit's seven-year term was punctuated by flawed strategy, questionable acquisitions, manufacturing controversies, and ethics scandals that jeopardized significant government contracts, costing the company billions of dollars, thousands of jobs, and a loss of reputation and trust that took years to rebuild.[3]

A top Harvard MBA graduate, Earnest Stanley O'Neal joined Merrill Lynch & Company as a junk-bond trader in 1986 and steadily advanced to become CEO in 2002. Intolerant of dissent and quick to take offense at perceived racial slights, O'Neal was a mercurial leader with an abrasive personality who had never worked as a stockbroker and had no particular affection for the business that had been Merrill's legendary mainstay for over 93 years. His burning ambition was to transform the Merrill culture into one that would take more and greater risks like his arch-competitor Goldman Sachs. O'Neal failed to realize that although Goldman Sachs took risks, they were measured risks and often based on consensus; O'Neal was adverse to collaboration at the executive level. His decisions alone were final.

O'Neal encouraged Merrill executives to accept more collateralized debt obligations backed by unstable mortgages, even when other firms were waking up to the high-risk dangers of excessive CDO exposure. In 2007, O'Neal resigned and, a year later, Merrill Lynch was purchased by Bank of America, in what many considered a fire sale of a cornerstone of Wall Street.[4]

Gerald Levin, chairman of Time Warner and Steve Case, chairman of AOL together spearheaded the largest corporate merger of the twentieth century and the supposed start of a new age where traditional media companies would work hand-in-hand with their internet rivals.

By the time the two companies formally combined in January 2001, it was clear to industry analysts and company officials that the cultural clash between the two organizations would prove insurmountable. Many who knew both CEOs noted at the time that the deal was motivated not by logic or sound strategy, but rather by the unbridled hubris of both leaders. The new company never really merged and neither company's initial strategy ever realized. Integration never took place—apart from at the corporate level. The failed megamerger ended up destroying over $200 billion in Time Warner shareholder value.[5]

Each of these CEOs was a bright, intelligent executive who clearly had the resume pedigree to be the top leaders of their respective companies. They each possessed measureable, demonstrable skills—whether as a brilliant engineer, confident risk-taker, or insurgent visionary. Observers familiar with these leaders have asserted that they each lacked the attributes that ultimately limited their success and brought about their failure—a deficient code of ethics, poor judgment, and the absence of humility.

Did anyone truly look into the substance of the individuals chosen to run these companies or the leaders of countless other companies who are falling short or failing every year because of an un-vetted character flaw or personal weakness? These examples are a microcosm of what is afflicting many organizations today: highly ambitious, competitive, often brilliant CEOs, abounding with skills, but all too often devoid of the consequential traits that constitute authentic, sustainable leadership.

## What Constitutes Success

Cultivating world-class CEOs abundant with skill *and* substance first requires the presence of a dynamic leadership development program that propagates the skills that advance the company's strategic plan. This allows board and management to define not only what success looks like, but the performance requirements expected of its leaders to attain and sustain that success.

Talent pipelines that consistently turn out great leaders require a broad and ongoing assessment of candidates in development.

This necessitates more than the design and involvement of HR, or the occasional oversight of the CEO or board. Thorough and robust assessments of successor capabilities require the involvement of multiple stakeholders and a variety of developmental actions, activities, and experiences purposefully orchestrated to maximize learning experiences.

While critical business skills and the demonstrable traits of strategic thinking, execution, and decision-making are essential dimensions of a successful CEO, over the years we've discovered deeper, less tangible patterns of traits that truly distinguish the more successful CEOs. Extraordinary leaders possess certain characteristics—attributes that have repeatedly proven instrumental in their effective and sustained leadership.

Boards can ascertain the presence of these character-defining traits by observing the behavior of each successor candidate through each of the following:

- Are they future forward—ensuring the right company strategy and direction?
- Do they make wise and principled investments of the company's resources?
- Do they achieve and sustain business results?
- Do they maintain an unwavering focus on employee engagement and talent development?
- Do they create customer and shareholder value?
- Do they maintain a consistent, moral landscape exhibiting courage, integrity, and high purpose?

Management psychologist Dr. Richard Davis defines these characteristics that are fundamental to executive success today as the "The Intangibles of Leadership," and includes among his list of required traits wisdom, will, executive maturity, integrity, social judgment, presence, self-insight, self-efficacy, fortitude, and fallibility.[6]

We believe these characteristics—though difficult to measure—are as important in grooming potential CEOs as are analytical and technical expertise, strategic thinking, decision-making, and execution.

The key insight here is that while tangible skills and experiences are certainly important elements to develop in CEO succession candidates, the intangibles that shape and define an individual's character are just as important in the thorough development of a company's leadership.

Unfortunately, the capturing and cultivation of these character-building traits are not part of the leadership development and succession-planning programs found in most organizations today. The problem is that many boards and CEOs believe they cannot adequately develop and measure the intangibles. And in some instances, companies caught unprepared and rushed to judgment because of the unplanned or sudden departure of a sitting CEO, are forced to pick a successor—many times external to the company—based solely on his or her functional capabilities. In their rush to judgment, there is little time to get to know the psychology of the person lying deep beneath the surface.

It is true that intangibles such as emotional intelligence, integrity, sound judgment, courage, and humility may be more difficult to capture and assess than the more observable skills that contribute directly to bottom-line results, but it's not impossible. In our practice, we have helped many boards and senior management teams learn to detect and develop these subtle traits in their candidates during character-building instances we call Moments of Truth—deep learning experiences captured and assimilated into a candidate's leadership development program through thoughtful reflection, mentoring, and coaching.

## MOMENTS OF TRUTH

The qualities of one's character are cultivated over many years through personal and business-related experiences. We believe these learning experiences—these Moments of Truth—help shape and build a candidate's personality. Being conscious of these teachable moments during the leadership development process and mindful of capturing and helping candidates reflect on and learn from these experiences can actually accelerate the cultivation timeline of top candidates.

Unfortunately, these critical traits are seldom if ever taken into account in the creation of a leader profile; nor are these intangibles sought after by search firms. When benchmarking external talent or executing a formal search, recruiters are primarily focused on definable successes and measurable achievements that match the inquiring company's strategic requirements. What are never on the radars of search firms are the intangibles of leadership: whether the candidate has relational skills, has shown integrity or fair judgment, is of moral and principled character, or has the ability to convey a vision and energize followers.

Many of the CEOs we've engaged with over the years relate to their Moments of Truth in different ways. Because of their positions of power, influence, and responsibility, most, if not all, experienced highly moving and intensely insightful occasions during their careers that cause them to think deeply about themselves, their values, and their style of leadership.

For many, these experiences forced executives to reflect on and reexamine their life and the beliefs, attitudes, and behaviors that have defined their leadership up through that instant in time. These moving experiences affected them personally, strongly contributing to the type of chief executives they eventually became.

Some could recall key turning points in their careers that brought about an immediate awakening or realization. For others, the process was more evolutionary, becoming clearer during the course of their careers. Some would have never recognized the lesson were it not for the feedback and insights of a significant other, a career mentor, or a trusted advisor who held a mirror up to them, helping them to reflect on a meaningful experience they would have otherwise failed to notice.

What the mirror reveals can sometimes be very complex, personal, and often troubling. But despite their different personal experiences, all agree that these Moments of Truth have the potential to be very constructive if boards, management, and CEO successor candidates could only take the time to capture, process, and integrate these experiences into their leadership development programs.

## MAKING THE DIFFICULT DECISIONS

Many people think that by the time executives reach the position of CEO, their education, training, and experience enable them to have a clear understanding of what they need to do in order to move a company forward. In reality, many chief executives purposefully project this demeanor as a defense mechanism or as a way to instill confidence in others. In our experience, however, a look behind the public image often reveals a degree of uncertainty. In exploring Moments of Truth with CEOs, some have recalled pivotal times in their careers when they were forced to contend with a critical decision or series of decisions without having any idea of how to proceed.

Shortly after joining Harnischfeger Corporation (later Joy Global) as president, John Nils Hanson discovered that the company's difficulties were so severe that the only solution was to declare Chapter 11 bankruptcy. As an astute businessperson, he never thought he would be in such a situation. The effect at the time was profound and unforgettable:

> You can't prepare for something like this and so it becomes a very deep kind of personal, emotional shock. It was probably the first time in my career where I had a sense of vulnerability. I don't mean that just in the sense that I might get fired, but the feeling that events may really be way outside of anything I could impact or control. Once the decision to declare bankruptcy was made, the situation quickly deteriorated as creditors focused solely on their personal short-term survival.
>
> The turning point came for me when I realized that my only choice was to focus on the one thing that mattered—the institution. In the end what worked for me was the fact that I stayed focused 100 percent of the time on what was good for the business. With this insight, I was able to take control and make the really difficult decisions. If I had been more focused on my personal concerns, the fears of one group, or the needs of one segment of the business, we would have simply fallen victim to the special interests who were trying to tear the whole enterprise apart. I had to remain above that—to keep my head up and vision forward.
>
> That risk is what turned a moment in my career into an amazingly useful learning experience. When I think back over my career to when I've seen constructive development take

place, it's usually where executives were thrown into a situation that was relatively undefined and difficult and then provided with just enough support and counsel to figure it out. Typically, those were the people who were able to gain the insight that allowed them to grow as leaders. I grew exponentially in my leadership as a result of my experience.[7]

Thanks to Hanson's efforts, the company remained intact. John continued on with the organization as chairman and CEO from 2000 to 2006. Today, Joy Global enjoys a market cap of nearly $8 billion and is the market leader in the mining machinery industry.

## CREATING TEACHABLE MOMENTS

John Hanson's Moment of Truth as president of Harnischfeger Corporation taught him invaluable lessons and honed his capacity and effectiveness in his years as chairman and CEO of Joy Global.

Hanson's learning experience had a profound effect on his approach to succession planning at Joy Global. Today, high-potential candidates in the company are identified and placed into rigorous leadership develop programs four to six years prior to the planned transition date. Over the course of that time span, the candidates with the most promise are tasked with heading up specific divisions within the company. These candidates also engage in formal and informal meetings with the board, giving directors an opportunity to get to know each one personally, to assess each of their functional capabilities, and to learn more of the leadership experience of each individual, gaining a sense of each candidate's judgment, integrity, humility, and relational skills.

The key insight here is intentionally designing character-building experiences into a company's leadership development and succession-planning program with increasingly challenging assignments that test not only their functional skills, but also reveal their character and personality traits to the board, senior management, and most especially to themselves.

These assignments must be meaningful and bear a real risk of failure to give board and management a full view what each candidate is capable of accomplishing under pressure. Such assignments will allow successor candidates the opportunity to discover more about their own behavior, judgment, and integrity under pressure—to hone their strengths and learn their weaknesses.

Giving a company's CEO successor candidates such stretch assignments creates teachable moments for them, elevating their leadership to a place they could never attain through the standard functional capabilities approach to pipeline development. This is how the best leaders are developed, for all levels within the organization, and the most capable leader as successor to the CEO discovered in the process.

We believe that to move from level to level is incremental, but in this global age, the move up to CEO is exponential. Merely *having* a talent pipeline is no longer a sufficient condition for an organization looking to achieve and sustain new levels of growth. The intensity and complexity of today's business environment requires a matching level of intensity and complexity in a company's leadership development and succession-planning program.

Those responsible for cultivating a company's leadership and identifying the individuals who have the ability to rise to the very top must create an experiential environment that goes far beyond the mere testing of business skills. Companies need to expose the depth and character of each of their successor candidates by creating teachable moments that expose the true substance of its future leaders and help boards and management together determine which candidate is best qualified in the long-run to lead the entire organization.

## CULTURES OF DEVELOPMENT

Companies that are able to continuously sustain their success and distance themselves from competitors exhibit strong cultures of development. Their boards and management, in genuine partnership, create a vision and strategic future for their organizations and are actively involved in the cultivation and advancement of their own leaders in the attainment of that future.

They maintain highly effective CEO succession planning programs that succeed at attracting and retaining valuable talent and create leadership development programs that accelerate the development of their high-potential employees through stretch jobs and assignments, offering the best training and the best opportunities for successor candidates to display their functional capabilities.

These companies not only develop the skills and abilities of their future leaders, but also shape and define the character traits that they expect their leaders to possess. In this fashion, the stretch jobs and assignments create teachable moments that reveal to board and management which candidate best exemplifies the ethics and values of their organization.

## Guiding Values

For two generations, Johnson & Johnson's management and educational training, as well as its specialized individual development programs, have consistently provided the company with managers and leaders ready to step in and fill key positions all over the world. Candidates are found in many of the 250 or so companies under the J&J corporate banner—individual profit-and-loss centers that provide the skill- and character-building testing grounds for future leadership talent. As a demonstration of Johnson & Johnson's succession planning competence, most of the company's CEOs, throughout its 125 years of operation, have risen from within the organization.[8]

At Johnson & Johnson, *The Credo*, a 60-year-old document, embodies the company's core values and outlines responsibilities toward customers, employees, community, and shareholders. Every major decision at Johnson & Johnson starts with alignment to *The Credo*.

*The Credo* also provides the foundation for leadership development at J&J. Based on the values described in *The Credo*, J&J created *The Global Standards of Leadership*, a document designed to provide the organization with guidance for both the performance evaluation of employees as well as for the development of its leaders. J&J's CEO William Weldon says, "There's forgiveness on the numbers side but not on the *Credo* values. Business results have to be tied to them."[9]

## Experiential Learning

Succession planning at IBM today is a best-in-class model of leadership continuity—at all managerial levels, and on every continent. Leadership development at IBM is a comprehensive, staged process owned by a fully engaged and strategically aligned board. A core responsibility of each leader in the organization is to identify and develop three to four successors—a selection not solely based on analytical skills or technical knowledge, but also on the way in which each high potential responds to character-building challenges as they move through various assignments within the organization.

On January 1, 2012, 30-year IBM veteran Virginia Rometty became CEO of IBM, succeeding Sam Palmisano, another career IBMer, who succeeded Louis Gerstner as CEO in 2002. In an interview, Rometty said she had received support and mentoring throughout her career at IBM by managers who wanted to see her succeed, and that she had grown most in her career through "experiential" learning. Rometty caught Palmisano's attention the year he became CEO when she helped integrate the $3.9-billion acquisition of PwC Consulting—IBM's largest deal ever at the time. Rometty said that she knew from the start the acquisition would be challenging, but that she had grown most in her career as a direct result of that experience.[10]

One of the most critical challenges facing companies today is in preparing each succeeding generation of leaders to be capable of extending the strategic reach of their organizations. The most successful companies are the ones that are in constant strategic renewal and alignment and regard the development of their executives and managers as an integrated part of company strategy. They create cultures of development that extend two or three levels deep into the organization, teaching and sustaining value-based performance at all levels.

Companies whose succession-planning programs create teachable moments that develop the character and integrity of their candidates continuously produce effective and successful CEOs who become rooted in who they are, what they stand for, and what they are capable of achieving. They gain self-confidence in knowing that they are not only doing things right, but doing the right things.

# Key Insights

✓ Talent pipelines that consistently turn out great leaders necessitate more than the involvement of HR, or the oversight of the CEO or board. Powerful assessments of successor capabilities and character require the involvement of multiple stakeholders and a variety of developmental actions, activities, and experiences purposefully orchestrated.

✓ While tangible skills and experiences are certainly important elements to develop in CEO succession candidates, the intangible attributes that shape and define an individual's character are just as important to nurture to insure the thorough development of a company's leadership.

✓ Emotional intelligence, integrity, sound judgment, courage, and humility can be detected and developed during character-building instances called *Moments of Truth*—deep learning experiences captured and assimilated into a candidate's leadership development program through thoughtful reflection, mentoring, and coaching.

✓ Intentionally designing character-building experiences into a company's leadership development and succession planning program with increasingly challenging assignments test not only functional skills, but also reveal the character and personality traits of the candidates to the board, to senior management, and most especially, to themselves.

✓ Companies whose succession planning programs create teachable moments that develop the character and integrity of their candidates continuously produce effective and successful CEOs who become rooted in who they are, what they stand for, and what they are capable of achieving. They gain self-confidence in knowing that they are not only doing things right, but doing the right things.

# SOURCE EXTERNAL TALENT AND MANAGE SEARCH FIRMS

## 10

*"Globalization has changed us into a company that searches the world, not just to sell or to source, but to find intellectual capital—the world's best talents and greatest ideas."*
—Jack Welch, former chairman
and CEO, General Electric[1]

There are clear advantages for companies that grow their own talent and cultivate each succeeding generation of leaders. They preserve their culture and maintain their strategic direction by perpetually and purposefully testing, developing, and advancing high potential employees within the organization. Successors with a history with their company also experience a much higher success rate and are significantly less expensive to hire when compared to externals. This is because they emulate the corporate culture and are knowledgeable of the company's people, values, and systems. And, over the course of their careers, their company's products, competitors, markets, customers, and suppliers become their worldview, and their industry, their field of play.

Yet, as with any organism or system, companies that have a long-standing history of success can become too self-confident and increasingly insular in their business plans and programs. There is a natural tendency for organizations, especially industry leading firms, to become complacent, relying too heavily on tried and true business practices and an implicit vision of the future. In this context, companies can unknowingly create inward-looking succession planning programs that identify and cultivate leaders who are skilled at working the system, but not experienced at challenging it.

Companies such as General Electric, Procter & Gamble, Johnson & Johnson, McDonalds, 3M, and Sony have learned not to propagate such insular thinking. They've successfully preserved their cultures and advanced their companies with each successive generation of inside CEOs by consciously seeding their leadership pipeline with external talent early in the succession planning process.

There are also times when the best CEOs can come from outside the organization, intentionally hired during a critical juncture in a company's history—a point in time when a shock to the system in the form of change leadership is required to regain that competitive edge.

## THE OUTSIDER ADVANTAGE

Albert Einstein once said, "You cannot solve a problem from the same consciousness that created it. You must learn to see the world anew."[2] This is the advantage of external talent, whether brought in at an early stage in the succession planning process or directly as the next CEO.

For an insider, rules and long-held assumptions are not only difficult to challenge, but often difficult to identify, because an insider is raised within the existing culture. Alternatively, an outsider, at any level of leadership, can bring an unemotional, unencumbered viewpoint necessary to challenge the way things have always been done. At the executive level, an external CEO can provide the opportunity to chart a new strategic course for the organization by pursuing new technologies, new products and services, unconventional markets, or to reenergize a corporate culture muddled in bureaucracy and contention.

This is not to say that the efforts of an outside CEO will be openly embraced. External talent often faces strong headwinds, especially when confronted with hardened corporate structures. For this reason, outside CEOs brought in as instruments of change need more than analytical skills and a unique vision of the future, for they are not just challenging processes, but also the resistant cultures that created them.

Outside CEOs, or for that matter, any external talent, must have the emotional strength and mental agility to deal with reluctance and resistance, to motivate internal stakeholders and gain their support and commitment. They must have the self-confidence and strength of conviction to withstand the skepticism of shareholders, analysts, media, and markets, and ultimately win their trust.

## Outsiders Challenge Organizational Hierarchies

A number of industries tend to focus on experience as a key to success, and the older the industry, the more valued one's experience within it. For decades, Detroit automakers have been managed by career car people, with virtually every senior management position filled by a 30- to 40-year veteran. When Mulally was brought in to run Ford, he didn't have years of experience in the automobile industry, and many constituents—from union workers, to senior executives, to shareholders, to industry analysts—predicted he would be run over within his first year.

While it's certainly true that experience is helpful, it's also true that too much of the same past experience can be detrimental. The reality is that Mulally had structural experience from his Boeing years that directly applied to Ford and automobile manufacturing, including long product lead times, cyclical product demand, union involvement, and an interconnected supply chain. What did make a difference was Mulally's energy and efficiency, his ability to help Ford regain its focus on the core business. He challenged organizational hierarchies that suppressed creativity and individual initiative. He concentrated on building teams before building cars. This outsider rekindled hope and vision at a most difficult time for Ford and for the automobile industry as a whole.[3]

## Outsiders View Problems Unemotionally

When IBM hired Lou Gerstner in 1993, the company needed more than a talented executive. It desperately needed a leader from outside the organization. For the first time in the company's 100-year history, IBM had hired a CEO who was not brought up through the corporate ranks. In his nine-year tenure as CEO, Gerstner lifted the company out of its organized chaos and restored it to its place as a computing powerhouse.

In his autobiography, Gerstner described the turnaround as difficult and often tortuous for an IBM culture that had become insular, bureaucratic, and antagonistic. After he arrived, over 100,000 employees were laid off from a company that had always maintained a lifetime employment practice that was now expected by its fourth generation of employees, regardless of accomplishment. Downsizing and other tough management measures continued in the first two years of Gerstner's tenure, but the company was saved, and IBM's business success has continued to grow steadily since.[4]

Finding and attracting talent such as Mulally or Gerstner doesn't come easy. Companies, faced with the need to benchmark external talent early in the succession-planning process, or rushed to conduct a formal search for a CEO, need external support. Boards, CEOs, and SVPs of HR simply don't have the time or the intelligence-gathering resources to know who is available and when. In this regard, search firms can be an invaluable resource for understanding the quality and quantity of external talent in the marketplace and helping to either seed the talent pipeline or find an immediate successor CEO.

## THE ROLE OF THE SEARCH FIRM

The best way to ensure that a company's leadership development and succession-planning program is dynamic and future leaning is to cultivate internal candidates who are not only the best and brightest within the company—but also the best and brightest within the industry.

This requires benchmarking the skills and accomplishments of external talent during the succession-planning process and using the intelligence gathered to augment internal training and development programs. The best entity to accomplish this task is the executive search firm.

Search firms can become a company's most valuable independent, intelligence-gathering resource when they are engaged well in advance of a transition date, truly understand the requesting company's strategic heading, and have a feel for the culture of the organization. The best search firms have long-standing partnerships with their clients developed over many years, giving search consultants context and an appreciation for the company's strategic future and culture.

Unfortunately, this is not when and how companies typically employ search firms. When engaging with executive recruiters, many companies prefer a short transaction relationship and expect recruiters to fade into the background until the next need arises.

Transactional searches do have their place, but this approach doesn't allow for the necessary depth of understanding that enables a search firm to identify an executive or CEO who is not only a strategic fit, but also a cultural fit. And as we've discovered, this lack of understanding invariably results in high CEO failure rates—often within the first 18 months of the new CEO's term of office.

In most instances, search firms are brought in at the eleventh hour in reaction to an unplanned CEO departure or dismissal. With their backs against the wall and the pressure to fill the position as quickly as possible, boards abdicate full responsibility to the search firm for evaluating and, in some instances, even selecting the successor CEO.

Dr. Harry Ashenhurst, retired chief administrative officer and COO of Lennox International, believes that, while an experienced search consultant can help identify qualified external candidates, the search firm must not be allowed to take over the process. Their role is to guide and facilitate the process on behalf of the board and it is ultimately the board's responsibility to select the proper candidate from the slate of internal and external talent provided.

> Opportunities are always far greater, broader, and deeper with known internal candidates. But, sometimes, boards and management are motivated to look outside the corporation for the next CEO and place a great deal of faith in what search firms can do in this arena. Boards need to be careful, because there are critical errors that can be made.
>
> When moving from an internal to an external search, time becomes a limiting factor and boards are inclined to minimize their involvement and engagement, allowing the search firm to lead and manage the process. The search firm will act as a

filter, and in doing so, limit the kinds of candidates brought to the table.

A board that gives their search firm the keys to the kingdom in this way and free reign in selecting the CEO successor is operating on a hero model that believes that if the company has the one right person in place, then all will be well. Boards that operate this way and do not involve all internal stakeholders in the succession process can end up paying dearly in the years to come.[5]

The best solution is to engage a search firm to benchmark external talent early enough in the succession-planning process—at least two to three years prior to the transition date. Then, if nine to twelve months out the board discovers that its internal candidates are not capable of fulfilling the top leadership position, the board has enough time to engage a search firm to conduct a formal search. This will give the search firm enough time to identify available talent, provide the board with options, and for the board to vet final candidates. And if an external successor is offered the position—most likely an existing officer of another company—that candidate will have time to evaluate and negotiate the offer and, if accepting, give adequate advanced notice before resigning his or her current post.

## Conflicting Interests

In addition to qualifying external candidates, search firms, increasingly over the past ten years, have offered to assist boards and CEOs during critical stages of the succession-planning process by assessing internal talent.

The key insight here is the potential conflict of interest in a search firm serving as an identifier and recruiter of potential candidates *as well as* an assessor of that talent. We feel that, while search consultants may be skilled at identifying potential candidates, a negative or even positive assessment of a candidate may appear to be—or actually be—self-serving.

A lawsuit was recently filed against one major search firm by an unsuccessful internal candidate who claimed that the search firm conducted an assessment of him, found him lacking, took him out of the running and then won the search assignment to replace him.

According to the lawsuit, the search firm had a personally vested, and therefore highly conflicting, interest in finding him *unqualified* to be promoted.[6]

Our message to boards is that the roles of identification and assessment of talent need are best maximized when separated. There are firms that are professionally educated and experienced in psychometric assessment. They can serve as a fair witness and facilitator to the board during critical stages of the succession-planning process by ensuring objectivity, maintaining transparency, mitigating emotionally charged issues, and benchmarking best practices in the talent development and succession-planning programs found in other organizations.

## External Pipelining

As we noted earlier, transactional executive search and placement have their value. But in this rapidly changing business environment, companies are increasingly looking to extract more from their relationship with their search firm. Many companies making a concerted effort to develop ongoing leadership development and succession planning are looking to invest in a talent-building source to address continuously their evolving business needs. As a result, they're asking for more and earlier involvement of search firms as a source of talent intelligence—to act as their company's external talent pipeline.

External executive pipelining is a process in which experienced executive search consultants identify, provide background information, and introduce an array of market talent in support of a client's needs. At the direction of the client, the team builds a pool of external talent based on selection criteria and a database of candidates are provided to the company to seed succession-planning programs long term and fill unplanned vacancies short term.

Robert Stein, founder and CEO of Prospect City, Inc., an innovator in external pipelining, knows the strengths and weaknesses of executive search firms, having been in the business for over 30 years. And Stein recognizes a growing desire on the part of boards and senior management to establish more involved and longer-term relationships with their executive search consultants.

An executive search is a lot like reaching into a fast-moving current and trying to catch a particular fish at that moment in time. It's a high-risk, time-sensitive engagement process, and the client assumes all the risk. That has been the nature of the executive search business since the 1950s and it hasn't changed much since then. The traditional search approach can only identify the fish swimming by at a particular time, and the candidates who can be introduced to companies are limited to those who are available at that moment.

There will always be companies that want the immediate transaction and are willing to pay for it, but an increasing number of boards and senior management are expressing their preference for longer-term planning and are looking to benchmark and compare the talent that's out there against the high potentials they're developing internally. They want to seed their internal succession-planning programs with either the skills and knowledge of the external talent, or with the talent itself. Pipelining approaches give companies a read on the fish up-river as well as those ready to be caught right now.[7]

External pipelining allows the board and senior management to lead the talent search and become familiar with the skills and performance levels of external talent, and ensure their internal talent development programs are building those skills and attaining those performance levels. It also enables board and management to identify external talent early in the leadership development process and integrate that talent into their succession-planning program, strengthening the bench of potential candidates years before the CEO transition date.

## Seeding the Pipeline

A critical difference between companies that manage succession well and those that don't is the understanding that succession is a process and not an event. And as we noted in Chapter 6, that process should begin years before the transition date of the sitting CEO.

Both internal and external talent have their strengths and weaknesses. Home-grown leaders have deep knowledge of the company, a sense of corporate history, and respect for the culture but often are desensitized to the need for fundamental change. External talent may bring fresh perspective, but lack the knowledge of the company's people, technology, competitiveness, and culture that are crucial for success. Moreover, the sudden integration of outside talent can undermine or disrupt the effectiveness of a sitting CEO or executive team.

What organizations need, then, is to purposefully seed the pipeline early in the leadership development and succession planning process with candidates who maintain an outside perspective. They have a deep understanding of the company, but are not afraid to question or challenge the status quo.

Harvard Business School professor Joseph Bower has done research that suggests that, as a rule, the best leaders are people from inside the company who have somehow maintained enough detachment from the standard procedures and traditions to maintain the objectivity of an outsider. Bower defines these individuals as "Inside Outsiders"—leaders who have grown professionally at the company, have developed an intimate understanding of the organization's culture, strengths, and weaknesses, yet have managed to remain objective about the organization's future.[8]

Jack Welch is an excellent example of an Inside Outsider. Welch spent his career at GE, earning a reputation as a strong and effective manager, but always considered himself—and was considered by others—to be a maverick. His background and demeanor reinforced his being labeled as a non-conformist given his Ph.D. in chemical engineering, background building GE's plastics business (not in GE's core), and assertive manner.

Nevertheless, Welch's unique perspective enabled him, within the first few years of his leadership, to dismantle and rebuild much of the staff and systems that his predecessor, Reginald Jones, had put in place. As CEO, Welch was viewed as a very aggressive agent of change, but as an Inside Outsider, he did it in a way that worked for General Electric. Welch was famous for demanding that every GE business be number one or number two in market share. If not, the company would "fix it, sell it, or shut it down." In a metric-driven company like GE, that clear market share directive provided an unambiguous challenge for the company's business leaders. During Welch's 20-year tenure as CEO, GE's market cap grew 6,000 percent.[9]

Inside Outsiders are purposefully seeded early in the succession-planning process and given increasingly challenging assignments outside the mainstream of the organization. In this fashion, they become familiar with the company's history, its people, processes, markets, competitors, and network of suppliers, but are still able to see the company with fresher eyes that haven't become habituated to the status quo.

Before becoming CEO, P&G's A.G. Lafley spent several years in Asia building the Chinese operation in beauty products rather than the core and very mature P&D detergent business, planning how to make P&G relevant in the twenty-first century when speed and agility would matter more than distribution and market muscle. As CEO, Lafley proved to be even more of a revolutionary than his predecessor, Durk Jager, leading the most sweeping transformation of the company since its founding by William Procter and James Gamble in 1837.[9]

Sam Palmisano, IBM's CEO from 2003 to 2011, was an early champion of software and open systems at a time when Big Blue was essentially a closed-system, hardware-oriented company. In 1988, he changed the way IBM sold computers—hardware with preprogrammed software—and his assertive approach to sales set the pattern for IBM's future. In 1991, Palmisano was sent to direct the operations of IBM Japan, where he gained a reputation for being a maverick who challenged the decisions of upper-level managers while frequently introducing innovative products to the Japanese market.[10]

Building a talent pool of Inside Outsiders requires a significant investment of money, time, and patience on the part of the company. Equally important, the incumbent CEO and executive team must not view the outsider's non-traditional ideas and methods as a threat but rather a future value. Mentors and sponsors need to recognize when a rising executive has a unique perspective and should encourage and nurture this quality over time through a carefully chosen sequence of assignments that builds and tests the capabilities of the external talent.

## Mentoring the Mavericks

Building a pipeline of future leaders begins with the board and senior management aligned on the future of the organization and their seeding the talent pipeline with candidates who are knowledgeable of the company and its culture, yet objective in their business processes and procedures and embracive of new technologies, emerging markets, and changing consumer demands.

Seeding the pipeline with external talent is not enough, however. The natural human inclination is toward conformity and hierarchy, and because of this predisposition, corporate cultures tend to suppress mavericks and nonconformists. Search firms may be able to identify and secure the best external talent, but that talent won't remain long if the corporate culture they're brought into is repressive to the point where the external talent either leaves in frustration or adopts the DNA of the company and becomes too much of an insider.

The most successful companies not only consciously seed their leadership pipeline with external talent early in the succession-planning process but also mentor and encourage that talent along with all the other mavericks and innovators found throughout the organization. Successful companies are forever mindful of the fact that everyone, at one time or another, was an outsider. Developing future leaders requires visionary boards and CEOs that establish cultures that embrace change and cultivate leaders who are skilled at both working the system and challenging the system for the better.

## Key Insights

✓ Companies can unknowingly create succession-planning programs that cultivate future leaders who are skilled at working the system but not experienced at challenging the system. Successful companies have learned to prevent such insular thinking by purposefully seeding the pipeline with external talent early in the succession-planning process.

✓ The best CEOs are not always insiders. There are times when the best CEOs can come from outside the organization, intentionally hired during a critical juncture in a company's history—a point in time when a shock to the system in the form of change leadership is required to regain that competitive edge.

✓ Search firms can become a company's most valuable independent, intelligence-gathering resource when they are engaged well in advance of a transition date, truly understand the requesting company's strategic heading, and have a feel for the culture of the organization.

✓ There will always be a potential conflict of interest when a search firm serves as an identifier and recruiter of potential candidates as well as an assessor of that talent. The roles of identification and assessment of talent need to be independent and unbiased to prevent any potential financial conflicts of interest.

✓ The most successful companies not only purposely seed their leadership pipeline with external talent early in the succession planning process but also mentor and encourage that talent. Developing future leaders requires visionary boards and CEOs that establish cultures that embrace change and cultivate leaders who are skilled at both working the system and challenging the system.

# SELECT THE CEO

# 11

*"If you pick the right CEO, serving on the board is actually pretty inter-esting and enjoyable. If you pick the wrong CEO, there are not enough board meetings and committee meetings to overcome that bad decision."*
—Charles Noski, vice chairman,
Bank of America Corporation,
former vice chairman,
AT&T Corporation

As we have cited numerous times throughout this book, it is our firm belief that the most important decision any board of directors can make is the selection of the CEO. Getting this decision right will have a significant impact on the trajectory and sustained success of an organization, while getting it wrong can set in motion a ripple effect of adverse consequences that can detract from positive growth.

Up to this stage, our Key Dimensions have built a solid founda-tion for succession planning and the developmental steps required to identify and cultivate a slate of candidates from which the board can confidently select its next top leader.

We spoke of how the succession planning process is best approached as a partnership between the board and CEO, how board and management must be aligned on the strategic direction of the organization, and how the strategic plan appropriately defines the requisite leadership requirements of the CEO and other company officers. We discussed how succession planning and development time frames should be purposefully extended to cultivate internal candidates and allow them the experiential time needed to mature as future leaders. We stressed why and when boards should take the opportunity to benchmark external talent to ensure their inside candidates are not only the best talent in the company, but the best talent in the industry. For our readers, we have laid out the steps that will effectively advance a board to the most important decision it will ever make as a governing body—selecting the next CEO.

Without question, planning for CEO succession creates the most advantageous environment for the continuous development of candidates who are ready to assume the reins of leadership. But making the final decision and selecting the CEO from a field of what may appear to be equally qualified candidates requires exceptional consideration. It demands a rigorous assessment process that will, in the end, enable the board to make an informed decision with the utmost confidence and to the greatest benefit of the organization.

## PREPARING FOR THE MOST IMPORTANT DECISION

Because of the critical value afforded a company when making the right decision, and the immeasurable cost for getting it wrong, the CEO selection decision must be grounded in a thorough and in-depth assessment of each candidate. The foundational guide for this entire assessment process is the Leader Profile, the blueprint that defines the requisite leadership skills and character traits expected of the successor CEO—the skills and traits that will strengthen the organization, engender the confidence and trust of all constituents, and ultimately deliver the strategic plan.

As Charles Noski so accurately observes in the quote above, board life can be heaven or hell depending on its decision as to who will lead the company into the future. The startling reality though is that boards consider themselves inadequate in making well-informed succession decisions. In our joint survey with *Chief Executive* magazine of 236 directors, we discovered that 60 percent of board members feel that their interviewing skills are deficient, and nearly half admit that they rely far too much on the candidate's resume.[1]

Candidates at this stage of their careers typically have a wealth of interview experience. They are so polished in their presentation and prepared in their responses that 40 percent of directors sense a lack of candor or authenticity during the actual interview process. Further, comparing an internal candidate with known imperfections to an experienced outsider with a seemingly clean slate can challenge almost any director. And even if sincere and forthright, the past experience of a candidate may not accurately predict how well that executive will fare in a different, uncertain, or highly challenging business environment.

Polished presentations and rehearsed responses provide nowhere near the information needed to assess a candidate, nor do resumes or letters of reference, which we will explore later in this chapter. This situation is exacerbated by directors having professional experience but not the capability to explore deeply enough what a candidate may bring to the table. Additionally, board members may have extensive industry experience as well as their own record of accomplishments as CEOs or corporate officers, but directors, relying on their own experience in assessing the capabilities of a candidate, should not be the sole determinant of an individual's future potential.

These uncertain issues require a more thorough analysis of successor candidates from trained, experienced, and unbiased professionals, who are independent from the search process, objective in their evaluation of each candidate, and free of conflicting interests. Candidate assessments conducted by outside professionals can offer invaluable insights into the quality and promise of high potential candidates and their actual ability to address the strategic and behavioral requirements of the CEO position. They can lend deep understanding of the complexities of human behavior in business settings and translate psychological perspectives into practical and strategic value.

Candidate assessments should examine the nominee's knowledge, skills, social intelligence, and other personal attributes in order to form a broad and deep picture of each potential successor's true and unvarnished value. Complex and often hidden characteristics such as personality and emotional stability are not easily identified in interviews, but nevertheless need to be taken into account and appraised accurately and judiciously through a professional assessment procedure. Given the level of inexperience in the interview and assessment process, board members benefit from the professional support in uncovering this level of insightful information through carefully scripted and meaningful interactions with each prospect.

## THE WINNING FORMULA

The assessment process must evaluate both the hard skills and technical requirements of the CEO position. Candidate evaluations must also measure the softer but equally critical leadership and character requirements that go a long way in shaping organizational culture, attracting and retaining talent, and enabling a leader to reach deep inside and govern with consistency and courage in times of crisis.

The Leader Profile outlines what it will take to be effective in the role of a CEO. This profile of leadership requirements—what we designate as The Winning Formula—provides the criteria or "template" against which boards can guide and assess the development of candidates who aspire to the role of top leader. The success factors as defined in the Leader Profile and the accompanying behavioral requirements are, in the end, necessary for the leadership success of a chief executive.

The context and content of the Leader Profile is developed through a series of interviews with the incumbent CEO and shaped by the elements of the strategic plan created by the board and CEO. The result, The Winning Formula for success in CEO succession, should include the following components:[2]

- *Industry Context and Operational Landscape*: The anticipated global economics; industry, consumer, and technology shifts; regulatory environment; competitive field of play; and social and political environments within which the company will operate over the next several years.

- **Business Strategy Overview**: Given the industry context and operational landscape, the issues, opportunities, and actions that the company and its CEO must address in order to achieve and sustain corporate growth over the next five to ten years.
- **Requisite Leadership Behaviors**: Considering the operating landscape and organizational imperatives in which the next CEO must function, the key role imperatives and requisite leadership behaviors critically important for the next CEO in strategy, execution, culture, talent, relationships with key stakeholders, board relations, and personal characteristics.
- **Desired Background and Experience of Succession Candidates**: Given the operating landscape and organizational imperatives of the company in the next several years, an initial list of relevant experiences that would be ideal for the next CEO to possess.

These elements are the quintessential role imperatives and requisite leadership behaviors expected of the incoming CEO—The Winning Formula that requires a rigorous assessment process in order to reveal the authentic substance of the candidate and ultimately guide a board to its final selection decision.

## THE INTERVIEW PROTOCOL

When Hewlett-Packard named Leo Apotheker as its CEO in 2010, the majority of the 12-member board that hired him had never interviewed or even met the former CEO of SAP, who was fired by the German software giant just a year earlier. Because of Apotheker's abrupt and unanticipated efforts to transform HP's strategic direction, the company's stock price plummeted 47 percent during Apotheker's short ten months in office.[3]

A board failing to interview—let alone meet—a successor CEO is an extreme example, but as we have shared in previous chapters, it's not unusual for boards to leave the succession decisions up to the sitting CEO, a search committee, or an external search firm. The reality facing many boards is that, even if they do interview the candidates, the interviews are not conducted with sufficient thoroughness to unveil all the information needed in order to make an informed succession decision.

In our experience, boards that make an effort to meet with CEO candidates may do so with the proper intentions but with insufficient time, process, and support. It's commonplace for candidates to spend one or a few hours with a board of directors in a formal or informal setting. But it's a bit superficial if all the board is accomplishing, given such limited time, is gauging the personality of the candidate and if he or she left a positive impression.

Since the board must live with their choice of successor for the months and years to follow, they owe it to themselves and their shareholders to invest time upfront to gain a deeper knowledge of the candidates themselves. Board members have to be more judicious in how they use that time with the candidates and what they want to discover or confirm in the strategic and behavioral competency of each individual. For that purpose, the Leader Profile serves as the ultimate discussion guide once developed into a behavioral assessment tool and process we call the Interview Protocol.

Once the board has ratified and signed off on the Leader Profile, the leadership requirements for the role of the CEO are customized into an Interview Protocol to yield behavioral insights into how a particular executive has performed in the past and is likely to perform in the future across the particular domains that are outlined in the Leader Profile.

The Interview Protocol contains a number of questions that may be used in the interviewing of candidates for the CEO position to determine if the aspirant possesses the requisite Behavioral Requirements, the capabilities and qualities necessary to succeed as CEO. The Interview Protocol is an effort to yield the data that will inform a judgment as to how that candidate stacks up to the leadership requirements.

If one of the behavioral requirements is the ability to think and act strategically, a director cannot simply ask the candidate if he or she is a strategic thinker, can translate complex issues into focused action, or is pragmatic in his or her decision-making. That simple line of questioning will reveal little more than yes or no answers with no depth of explanation or opportunity for follow-up probes. A properly developed interview guide will shed more light on the ability of the candidate to think and act strategically and, for that particular behavioral requirement, will include the kinds of probing questions found in our Interview Protocol.

## Interview Protocol Sample

### Behavioral Requirement 1: Problem-Solving and Thinking

**Components:**

- Ability to think both strategically and tactically
- Grasp of business issues and corporate/organizational functions
- Ability to translate complex issues into focused action
- Engages key stakeholders in addressing critical issues
- Pragmatic judgment in decision-making

**Questions:**

- In your most recent position, what was the most complex problem or issue that you confronted and how did you go about understanding and resolving it? What was the outcome of these efforts? What might you have done differently?
- Please share your thinking with us regarding the major social, technological, business, and/or political dynamics that will have the greatest impact on your industry in the next five to seven years.
- Please provide an example of where you had to develop a strategy for accomplishing a critical objective. What was the situation, how did you do it, and how has it unfolded?
- How do you go about learning something completely new? Please provide an example of when and how you accomplished this.

The components that comprise this and each of the Behavioral Requirements explored in the Interview Protocol are collected at the end of the interview guide in the form of a scorecard template to facilitate the comparison-rating of candidates for discussion and evaluation after the interviews.

Finally, the Interview Protocol should contain questions designed to help boards assess the ethics and integrity of each candidate. Again, an interviewer cannot simply ask a candidate if he or she has a code of ethics or integrity of purpose. All the director may receive is a yes or no answer. The candidate can provide a more robust and telling response by reflecting on past, current, or future scenarios.

---

## Interview Protocol Sample

### Ethics and Integrity Assessment

- What are the ethical dilemmas that are present in your current work context?
- Describe a time when you felt a conflict between multiple priorities. What were they and what was your thinking process as you decided what to do?
- As an executive, what, if anything, have you done to establish ethical conduct as a core value in the culture of your organization?
- Have you ever had a direct report, boss or colleague engage in questionable conduct that you felt it a duty to address? What were the situations and what did you do?
- What are the ways you would raise the bar on standards for ethical conduct if you were to lead this organization?

---

## Cautionary Note on Comparative Tests

In addition to the customized Interview Protocol, there are empirically derived assessments of cognitive ability and personality that are useful in augmenting interview data. These tests are given to candidates to benchmark them against all other executives against a particular type of role or function.

For example, if a company is engaged in a search for a CFO, there are questionnaires used by search firms that will test candidates against a pool of hundreds of other CFOs to benchmark how a particular CFO candidate matches against best-in-class CFOs on elements such as strategic thinking, financial acumen, or risk and asset management.

Although these tests claim to yield objective analysis and comparison and may provide compelling information, they tend to create a false sense of validity. Situations change, and as candidates are compared across industries, across companies of different sizes, and across different strategic contexts, such variables can quickly dilute the predictive value of the information provided. There's value in using empirically objective measures to complement the interview-based data that's gathered. However, these instruments should not take the place of actual in-depth interviews using the context and requirements of the Leader Profile when assessing each particular candidate.

## UNEARTHING THE BEST REFERENCES

Once the board begins to zero in on a candidate and feels that person can be a very good fit for the position, directors will ask the successor for references as one of the last steps in the assessment process. Typically, candidates are asked to supply the names of several individuals whom the board may contact as performance and character references to ensure truthful confirmations of everything learned during the interview process. There are various perspectives on the value of reference checking. Some believe it's the most important part of the recruitment process, arguing that the single best indicator of how a candidate will perform in the future is how they have performed in the past.

Others contend that references are of little value since a candidate will invariably stack the deck in their favor, offering the names of individuals who have strong ties and often personal relationships with the candidate—carefully chosen sponsors whom the candidate has already spoken with and confirmed their positive support. A candidate will seldom, if ever, offer the name of someone as reference without knowing that that person will give nothing short of a glowing testimonial. Nevertheless, references, if carefully extracted, can yield a wealth of valuable information.

## Customized Reference Checking

The referencing process should systematically address both functional and behavioral leadership requirements, and not just ask general questions about the candidate. References should include a cross-section of supervisors, peers, and direct reports whom have worked with the candidate and not be limited to the three to four names provided by the candidate.

We believe that the list of individuals to be solicited as references should emanate from a discussion with the candidate that exposes all of the parties who were stakeholders in the candidate's last two or three positions. By using the Interview Protocol, well-developed questions will bring to the surface names and situations that can support the identification of references.

In the case of CEO successor candidates, boards will interview candidates who may have held their current position for several years, but the acquisition of references should hold no smaller value. Best practice is to talk to the candidate and generate a list of references as a result of that discussion. As example, interviewing a CFO to determine the identity of the audit chair, the board chair, the CEO, the treasurer, or controller of the candidate's previous employer will ultimately reveal critical functional role partners, several of whom will become invaluable references.

Valuable information most always emerges during an interview process where candidates disclose, through situational anecdotes, the identity of stakeholders whom they engaged with in day-to-day operations as opposed to referring to peers, colleagues or association members who, 99 percent of the time, will be in support of the candidate. Directors are best equipped when they select references not according to what the candidates provide, but rather from the names of stakeholders that surface in such reference discussions.

Equally revealing is, during reference discussions, the raising of an objection from the candidate to a stakeholder as reference. This represents an opportunity for the board to explore the foundations of the candidate's objection. Sometimes the objection may be for a very good reason, but even the objection, in itself, will yield valuable information.

Once an appropriate list of references is identified, in-depth reference calls can be made using the leadership requirements from the Leader Profile to guide the inquiry. Rather than general questions and responses about the candidate, the referencing process should be a specific discussion of the candidate's capabilities and track record relevant to the Leader Profile for the CEO position that was ratified by the board. This approach yields much better information about how a candidate fits with the unique leadership context for this particular CEO selection.

After all the data is gathered from the board interviews, outside assessment process, and referencing, the full board should discuss how each of the final candidates matches the leadership requirements and identify the inevitable gaps that will exist. In some situations, the board may conclude that none of the candidates is satisfactory and a decision may be made to source additional candidates. That course of action takes considerable courage and conviction of purpose as there are often personality issues and organizational constraints that must be managed.

In the end, it is far better to take whatever time is necessary to ensure an optimum fit than to settle on a less than satisfactory or questionable candidate. As Stephen Patrick, retired vice chairman of Colgate-Palmolive Company, and current director of Arrow Electronics noted, "If you put the wrong person in the job, he or she can destroy 50 years of good work by the company and the board overnight."[4]

## ONCE THE SELECTION IS MADE

After the board reaches consensus about the selection decision, it is important for board and management to develop communication, transition, and integration plans. We cannot overemphasize how important the communication, transition, and integration management steps are to a comprehensive and effective CEO succession process.

We will address these elements in the following chapters, including: giving special attention to the role of the outgoing CEO in transitioning in the new CEO; the retention and continued engagement of the unsuccessful candidates who are critical to the future of the organization; and informing external stakeholders through a well-timed and well-crafted communication plan.

## Key Insights

✓ Because of the importance and the enormous cost of getting it wrong, the selection decision must be grounded in an extremely thorough assessment of final candidates against the leader profile.

✓ The assessment process needs to assess both the hard/technical requirements of the position and the "softer" but equally critical leadership and character requirements that shape organizational culture, attract and retain talent, and lead consistently and courageously in times of crisis.

✓ An external, professional assessment can provide invaluable insights about the candidates and their fit with the CEO position requirements, lend deep understanding of the complexities of human behavior in business settings, and know how to translate that psychological perspective into practical and strategic value.

✓ While use of an outside professional assessment process is advised, the board needs to invest sufficient time to get to know final candidates themselves as they will have to live with their succession choice. Best practice dictates boards use an in-depth interview protocol derived from the Leader Profile to acquire an in-depth knowledge of the final candidates.

✓ The referencing process should systematically address leadership requirements, not just ask general questions about the candidates. References should include a cross section of supervisors, peers, and direct reports who have worked with the candidate, not just the three to four names provided by the candidates.

# PROACTIVELY MANAGE THE TRANSITION

## 12

*"It's awkward and somewhat painful to turn over the reins to the new leader after you've been the CEO. The challenge is in transitioning what you know, then getting out of the way. If you don't get out of the way, you're ultimately in the way."*
— Brad Anderson, former chairman and CEO, Best Buy Co., Inc.

After having spent months deliberating over the final roster of CEO candidates and deciding on the company's next leader, boards tend to breathe a collective sigh of relief in the belief that their hardest work is behind them. Relieved, they will shift their focus to other pressing matters as they await the date of transition when the new CEO officially assumes office.

But the reality is that the board's work is far from over, because choosing the next CEO is actually the first step in transitioning a company's leadership. How that exchange is orchestrated over the ensuing months can be a positive or negative experience for the organization and conceivably affect the success or failure of the incoming CEO very early on in his or her term of office.

It is our view that the CEO transition period begins when the board makes its final decision on who the next leader will be and continues through the first two years of the new CEO's term of office. How long that integration period extends into the new leader's administration is conditional upon a number of factors that will be discussed later in this chapter.

We believe the events surrounding a transition of leadership fall into two stages: Stage 1 begins the moment the succession decision is made and ends when the incumbent CEO transfers leadership to the new CEO; Stage 2 is marked by that first day of the new CEO's term of office.

These stages are so closely aligned and necessarily seamless that we feel it best to address this continuum from "hand off" to "hands on" as one chapter in our book to emphasize the continuity in and entirety of that process.

## Stage 1: Transitioning the Organization

All too often, CEO transition is treated as an isolated event rather than an organizational process involving a host of constituents and activities insufficiently planned for or simply overlooked. In the weeks and months leading up to the new CEO assuming office, getting the transition right or wrong can have an immediate effect on organizational performance, share value, and market position.

A poorly orchestrated transition can diminish an otherwise-stellar tenure by the outgoing CEO and cause the company to feel uncertain about the competence or intentions of the new leader. And regardless of how appropriate the selection of the successor, poor planning can galvanize investors and the marketplace to question the strategic direction and resolve of the company.

Alternatively, a well-orchestrated transition can have significantly positive effects on the organization—from retaining top talent to infusing employees with renewed confidence, conviction of purpose, and accelerated momentum.

In our experience, transition success or failure—or the mediocrity that lies between—is a straight line to the board's awareness of the details following a selection decision and its attentiveness to the needs and expectations of a wide range of constituents. Interestingly, directors and CEOs have very different perceptions about the consideration and support required.

Research shows that directors generally have a favorable impression of how well their companies have conducted past CEO transitions. Studies indicate that 60 percent of board members feel satisfied with the results, stating that prior transitions under their governance have adequately met their expectations.[1]

However, the majority of respondents to our recent study on CEO transitions do not necessarily agree. Less than 40 percent of recently appointed CEOs claim that their board's involvement in the transition met their needs and expectations.[2] The majority of CEOs in our study recalled that the level of board support in their transition was inadequate and contributed to a more challenging transfer of responsibility and difficult first months in office.

The insight here is the type and degree of involvement that CEOs expect of their boards. CEOs are not advocating that their boards micromanage every element of the transition process, but rather that directors be attentive to organization dynamics, ask the right questions, and ensure that the needs and expectations of stakeholders, both inside and outside the firm, are being addressed—all to ensure the uninterrupted continuity of business. This underlies the reason why we consider this a transitioning of the organization and not just of the CEO.

Boards that properly play a strong, supportive role during the transitioning process, focus their attention on the critical areas that are sometimes insufficiently attended to or often completely overlooked during a transition of leadership, including:

- Managing the dynamics between the outgoing and incoming CEOs to ensure a smooth and thorough transfer of knowledge and enable the new CEO to establish his or her own presence of leadership.
- Making every effort to retain top talent, especially CEO candidates unsuccessful in their bid for the top leader position, but nevertheless crucial, to the future success of the organization.
- Developing and releasing a well-timed communications plan with a consistency of message that maintains employee focus and motivation and reinforces shareholder and marketplace confidence.

## Managing the Dynamics between the Outgoing and Incoming CEOs

The central goal in Stage 1 of transitioning leadership is ensuring that the transfer of knowledge, responsibilities, and relationships is accomplished without interrupting the focus and momentum of the organization. The challenge to that goal is in navigating the personal emotions and interpersonal dynamics that can impede the process and disrupt an otherwise-smooth transition.

Directors may show proper foresight and execution in the activities surrounding the transition process, but may find that the transfer of leadership itself is not going as well as planned, simply by failing to recognize and negotiate the undercurrent of emotions of the outgoing and incoming CEOs.

The outgoing CEO may be experiencing the fear of loss of power, the loss of association with peers, or the loss of personal identity with the company itself. The exiting leader may feel unappreciated for all that was accomplished during his or her term of office and may even disagree with the new CEO's initial decisions and new directions. These deeply personal emotions, often difficult for an accomplished executive to share, can create reluctance on the part of the outgoing leader to surrender power, protract the transfer of authority, undermine relationships with key constituents, or even negatively affect the momentum of the company.

Incoming CEOs experience their share of emotions as well. Often, there is great excitement and a desire to make a strong impact from the outset. For some, it may be the anxiety brought on by a fear of failure or errors in judgment during the transition period that might result in the new CEO getting off on the wrong footing with the board, the executive team, key customers, investors, analysts, or the media.

Conversely, incoming CEOs may overestimate their own skills or underestimate the scope and complexity of the job and attempt to do too much too quickly. Then there are those who may be immediately seduced by the power of the position and the unconditional adulation of others—a temptation that can transform personalities or weaken a leader's integrity, ethics, or purpose.

Aside from personal sentiments, there are also the interpersonal dynamics between the outgoing and incoming CEOs. Potential feelings of resentment are common for both parties: the outgoing CEO may feel as if the incoming leader is trying to change things too soon, and the incoming CEO may feel that the departing leader is unwilling to relinquish power. This dynamic is particularly true if the outgoing CEO, intent on shoring up his or her own personal legacy, remains on the board for an extended period in order to influence strategic decisions. On the other hand, many incoming CEOs recognize and value the considerable insight and perspectives of their predecessor and want to leverage that experience. Perhaps this range of feelings explains the almost even split among CEOs surveyed on the question of whether the outgoing CEO should remain on the board.[3]

To ensure a successful transition of leadership, these powerful psychological dynamics require attentive and unwavering oversight, wisdom, and judgment on the part of the lead director or non-executive chair. At the very least, a watchful eye should be kept on the outgoing CEO's needs and feelings; at the very most, a trusted mediator should intervene in the transfer of leadership and the interactions of the outgoing and incoming CEOs.

Allowing these psychological forces to play themselves out without some level of guidance can prove detrimental to the organization. The outgoing CEO needs to interact with someone he or she can openly confide in. And the new CEO can benefit from the coaching and guidance of a trusted lead director—a relationship that, at best, will continue to grow throughout the new CEO's term of office.

## Overlapping Leaders

There are some instances when a clean break between the incoming and outgoing CEO is best for the organization. There are other situations and environments where the overlapping of leaders for a brief period is invaluable to ensure business continuity and momentum.

The best of all situations is when an outgoing CEO remains on for a brief transitional period after the announced succession and contributes to the success of the incoming CEO by orienting the new CEO to how the board operates and what pressing issues loom on the horizon. The outgoing leader can also help personally and visibly transfer to the new CEO external relationships with customers, suppliers, investors, analysts, and the media.

The outgoing CEO can also share his or her insights on the talents and skills of the individuals who make up the executive team and identify which of those individuals stand the best chance for becoming the company's future leaders. Conversely, the outgoing CEO can deal with personnel issues such as making decisions on moving out poor performers but leaving the selection of replacements to the new CEO.

The question of how long an overlap of leadership—optimally 3 to 12 months—is conditional upon the chemistry between the two executives, the definition of roles during the transition, and the complexity of the business. A textbook example follows below.

### A Masterful Transition

Ajay Banga left Citigroup and joined MasterCard as president and chief operating officer in late August 2009. Eight months later, in April of 2010, MasterCard announced that Banga would succeed Robert Selander as president and CEO effective July 1, 2010.[4]

As CEO of Citicorp's Asia-Pacific region, Banga built a wealth of experience in diverse industries and contrasting geographies—knowledge and maturity that MasterCard needed to strengthen its own global competencies and compete in the worldwide acceleration of electronic payments.

MasterCard's masterful transitioning of Ajay Banga into the organization was part of a three-stage plan created by Robert Selander to allow Banga to settle into the company and learn the business and culture without the burden of all the external and internal pressures that immediately befalls an incoming CEO.

The first stage was for Banga, as COO, to report to Selander. For one year in that capacity, Banga visited virtually every regional office to meet in-country leaders, study operations, and gain first-hand knowledge of MasterCard's obstacles, strengths, and resources at the country level.

The second stage was for Banga to assume the role of president and CEO, with Selander serving as the company's executive vice chair. The intention was for Selander to overlap Banga for six months through to the date of Selander's departure in December 2010, which completed the third stage of the transition plan—Banga as CEO with Selander in retirement. The transition was managed extremely well by both Selander and Banga and enabled the organization to catapult forward. MasterCard's stock price and market capitalization has more than doubled since the succession transition.

## Retaining Top Talent

One of the most unfortunate outcomes of selecting the CEO from a field of internal candidates is the risk that the other high potentials who may have spent months or years advancing in their leadership development—and in the process becoming indispensable to the organization—may choose to leave.

The board and senior management must be mindful of the need to preserve the company's top talent during and following the transitioning of leadership. Their focus must be on maintaining the unity and commitment of the executive team and ensuring that the remaining succession candidates, though unsuccessful in their bid for the top leader position, stay on with the organization.

Boards cannot guarantee that they can retain a candidate who has lost the chance to become CEO. For those candidates who do decide to leave, it often comes down to personal ambition rather than any fault of the succession process itself. There may be very strong emotions to contend with involving pride, the embarrassment of failure, or an impatience on the aspirant's part to accept any outside offer in order to move onward and upward.

Nevertheless, a company should make every effort to retain valuable talent. It is careless and wasteful to have invested years cultivating future leaders only to have them leave at the peak of their careers when attentiveness and honest dialogue may have been all that was needed to retain those executives.

Best practice is to treat the retention of top talent as on ongoing process. Ideally, CEOs and boards have deep knowledge about each candidate, years in advance of the transition date. Understanding the aspirations, motivations, and values of all top company executives is an ongoing responsibility of the CEO and HR. Boards should be briefed about potential succession candidates on at least an annual basis and have direct involvement with those candidates.

Equipped with that knowledge, boards should devise retention plans with mechanisms such as equity, compensation, or challenging assignments that will incent unsuccessful candidates to continue to advance their careers within the company. Challenging offers can be made to candidates to help lead the company in new technologies, spearhead new lines of business, or expand the firm's presence in emerging markets.

Once the selection decision is made, directors should engage in honest and open conversations with unsuccessful candidates about why they didn't get the job and what career development opportunities are still available to them. Although these discussions may be uncomfortable, they can increase the likelihood that a valued executive can be held onto and given a mission-critical role to play in the company.

## Proactive Communications Plan

Leadership change always affects a company's value. Whether that value change is positive or negative depends largely on the clarity, consistency, and credibility of the information shared by the board and senior management in the months, weeks, and days leading up to the date of transition.

When the information flowing from a company is inconsistent from one source to the next, or when little to no information is released, internal and external stakeholders may view the change with skepticism. They will invariably listen for what is not being said, piece together what they think is the intent of the company—including its stability and direction—and arrive at their own conclusions.

Constituents will want to know why there is a change in leadership at this time. They will want to know what will happen to the outgoing CEO—especially if the departing leader is an admired and respected figure. Many will be anxious to learn if there will be further changes to the senior management team or if there will be deeper personnel cuts or a possible restructuring of the organization. Stakeholders will be interested in the profile of the new company leader—his or her character, personality, intelligence, and temperament. And shareholders will most especially want to know if the incoming CEO will maintain or alter the strategy and direction of the company in the months to follow.

Once the board selects the new CEO, best practice is to construct a communications plan, endorsed by the board, the outgoing CEO, the incoming CEO, and the senior management team. The communication plan should identify the organization's key stakeholders and determine what exactly should be communicated to each group, by whom, and in what time frame.

Best practice is to have one source for all the information involving the transition including background on the incoming CEO, the status of the outgoing CEO, the actual transition date, and constancy in the strategic direction of the company. One message from one official source significantly reduces the chance for unfounded rumors, special interests, or confidential information to distort the message and undermine the transition process.

Not having a communication plan that provides clarity and consistency of message can negatively affect the market value of an organization by giving shareholders, investors, and analysts the impression that the company may not have a viable successor, or that there may be divisiveness and power struggles among board members or between board and management. The perception of disorganization can also severely undermine a company's ability to retain key executives, maintain company momentum, or recruit exceptional talent into the organization.

## Mixed Messages

Avon Products is an example of a company in the midst of leadership transition. At the time of writing, the company is challenged in presenting one unequivocal directional voice to its internal and external constituents. Consider the spate of contradictory messages released by Avon's board and senior management, including its past CEOs, all within a very tight window of time and all made so very public.

With a 45-percent decline in stock value in 2011, slowness to develop key emerging markets, and a developing SEC bribery probe, Avon's sales representatives, investors, and analysts have pressured the board to replace its long-standing CEO, Andrea Jung. Avon responded by announcing that in 2012, the company will separate the roles of chair and CEO—at Jung's insistence—and that Andrea

Jung, Avon's chair and CEO since 1999, will remain on as executive chair for two additional years.[5]

Immediately following that announcement, former Avon CEOs David Mitchell and James Preston released their own statements to the press, individually criticizing Jung's leadership. They both expressed concern that her decision to split the CEO-chair structure so she could remain on for two more years as executive chair was a poor decision that would make the board's search for a quality successor virtually impossible.[6]

Undaunted, Andrea Jung's internal letter released to all U.S. employees and global managers and made public through the *Wall Street Journal*, indicated that she doesn't plan to cede much power at all. Jung made it clear that she plans to remain very close to the business, defining the company's strategy and brand positioning as well as influencing the selection of the next CEO who, Jung insists, must be a woman.

In a concurrent statement to the media, lead independent director Fred Hassan, who is heading the search committee, confirmed that Jung will help the board's search committee but will lack the power to veto its recommended CEO pick, adding that "the board will get very good candidates from all over and won't limit its search to female candidates."[7]

In the absence of message clarity and consistency, the marketplace is left to conclude that Avon's external search will take months, the CEO transition itself will be a challenging process, and the process will be a long-suffering one before the new executive chair, the board at large, and the incoming CEO, develop and agree to a new strategic plan. What may unfortunately suffer the most in this volley of mixed messages are a company's share value, momentum, and ability to hold on to its top talent.

## Stage 2: Integrating the New CEO

Once the mantle of leadership is passed to the new CEO, integration takes center stage. Attentiveness shifts to the activities of the new leader—maintaining organizational momentum, establishing critical relationships with key stakeholders, achieving clarity on the strategic priorities of the organization, and becoming familiar with the people, issues, and problems that must be addressed.

In this fast-paced and highly complex business environment, new CEOs have a very short time in which to establish themselves and prove their value to the organization. Our research shows that, in the first three months that comprise the honeymoon period, many CEOs feel that they are all alone, and more than half stated that they received very little role clarity from the outgoing CEO, and just as many conceded that their boards offered insufficient support.[8]

## The Critical First Three Months

The integration of a new CEO occurs in predictable stages with success or failure determined primarily by what occurs in the first three months in office. A foremost determinant of success is the ability of the new CEO to establish a strong alliance and productive working relationship with the board, a most pivotal stakeholder group with whom the new CEO must forge a constructive partnership.

Some would contend that a strong partnership with the executive team is the key determinant of success, given that the senior staff is the group that will ultimately help formulate and execute corporate strategy. Nevertheless, the issues that cause new CEOs to derail and fail early in their term of office result from misalignment and interpersonal problems with their board formed within the first 90 days.

Our research shows that CEOs are acutely aware of the need for board alignment and support early on in their administration. They cite personality clashes, disagreement on corporate strategy, and transparency issues with directors as the types of issues that will more likely bring about their failure in office than similar issues with the senior management team.

Research conducted by authors Thomas Neff and James Citrin also define the first 100 days as a make-it-or-break-it period for a new CEO in terms of learning, adjustments, and setting of agendas, and that there are three common mistakes often made in this honeymoon period that can work against the new leader's succcess.[9]

The first mistake is for the CEO to fall into the trap of believing that he or she must have all the right answers from day one, particularly if the new leader is an outsider, brought in for the sole purpose of restructuring the organization.

The second is creating unrealistic expectations of what can be accomplished in a given time frame. New leaders, looking to make a name for themselves early on in their administration, create instead a treadmill of unsustainable expectations and push the organization too hard to achieve results.

The third mistake is to openly criticize the previous administration in terms of its leadership and strategic direction. Discrediting a previous leader will invariably create ill will among employees, key customers, and other stakeholders who may have been loyal to the past CEO or departing senior executives.

In our experience, beyond forming a constructive partnership with the board and executive team, there are specific actions that a new CEO must take in the first three months of office to increase the likelihood of success. The first is to create high visibility and communication of intent. This is the period when the new CEO must make important contacts with every critical stakeholder group, offering reassurance and establishing confidence. The new CEO must convey a genuine willingness to listen and learn and convey his or her integrity and trustworthiness—the most enduring leadership traits in this constantly changing global economy.

Our belief is that a most important activity for a new CEO to engage in during the first three months of office is to meet all the important stakeholder groups, not as a speaker, but as the audience. His or her genuine intent must be to listen to and understand the organization through the eyes of employees, customers, suppliers, investors, and other stakeholders. We believe that this early and visible behavior on the part of a new leader conveys a very powerful and important psychological message that says, "I'm new in this role and I don't want to pretend I have all the answers. I value your input."

Unless the new CEO is inheriting an organization that requires immediate hands on management, dedicating the first few months to absorbing all the input possible will ultimately help the incoming CEO, for the approach is more than symbolic. A new leader can acquire powerful information that can shape a better agenda, gain the support and trust of all constituents, and still leave the CEO in the position to do what he or she decides.

Once the new CEO becomes familiar with the people, issues, and problems that need attention, the leader must begin to reveal his or her strategic vision, competence, and signature of leadership. Major personnel and structural issues must be addressed, and the new CEO must begin to take steps in establishing his or her own agenda and mapping the strategic direction and alignment of the organization.

## When the Honeymoon Is Over

While the first three months are critical for a new CEO to learn about the organization, develop relationships, unveil his or her vision, and achieve early wins, an executive's integration does not necessarily stop at that point. Our research confirms that successful integration may extend well into the first two years in office, depending upon circumstances confronting the new leader and the company.[10]

There are instances when the important work of integration can resolve itself within months, and there are times when a new leader's assimilation may take much longer. There are situations where the incoming CEO, if an insider, may have served in transition, knows the strategic direction of the organization and is aligned with its people and culture. This may even include an Inside Outsider brought in for an extended period before becoming CEO with the intention of succession. The result is a seamless transfer of leadership.

In other instances, there may be a great deal of organizational upheaval resulting from a large acquisition or the merger of two organizations, and it could be one to two years before the reorganization is complete. In these and similar situations, it may take just as long for the integration of the new CEO to be considered complete.

It is important that boards not assume that the standard honeymoon period of 90 days is a sufficient amount of time for a new CEO to acclimate and begin to show results. Directors must be attentive to the support the new leader may require as dictated by the dynamics of the organizational environment, the market environment that may be driving strategic change in direction, and the competence environment – the ability of the firm to meet objectives.

We are not suggesting that boards be overly hands-on and controlling of every aspect of the new CEO's integration. We are suggesting, though, that directors be actively engaged as thought partners and as resources to the new leader. Moreover, we are not suggesting that the board solely focus on the personal integration of the CEO to ensure his or her effectiveness, but to be supportive of the ongoing effectiveness of the organization and the alignment of the executive team during the integration process.

## An Interrelated Process

As we stated at the onset of this chapter, a CEO transition involves far more than the transfer of power and responsibility from one CEO to the next. It is rather a systematic, pivotal inflection point in the history of the organization that involves three interrelated domains including the *individual,* the *organization,* and the *senior management team*—each requiring a thorough, well planned, and integrated approach. A thorough and successful integration addresses all three domains as an interrelated process with the intent of ensuring business continuity and organizational success.

Figure 12.1: The Three Interrelated Domains

### Individual Transition

The board can best support a thorough and successful transition by constructing a documented plan designed to assist the CEO during the first year in office. This detailed plan conveys the role requirements and expectations of the new leader and helps to accelerate his or her transition into the role of CEO.

The intent of the plan is to ensure a seamless transition of duties from the outgoing to the incoming CEO and defines the comprehensive business strategy that will sustain the momentum of the organization while the new CEO gains hands-on experience. Such a plan may also include an overview of each member of the executive team, outlining responsibilities, strengths, and weaknesses. The plan may also include a high-level profile of key internal and external stakeholders, a "First 90-Days" calendar of events, and a board of directors meeting schedule.

## Organizational Level Change

Paralleling the CEO's understanding of the personal roles and requirements needed to sustain the momentum of the organization, the CEO must assess the current state of the industry and competition, the strategic direction of the company, and if the culture, structure, and resources of the organization are aligned to that strategy.

The importance of this initial assessment of organizational effectiveness is to help the new CEO focus on the important, high-level issues that require support, change, or restructuring. This strategic overview will also help the new leader engage in effective change initiatives that will yield a positive impact with limited disruption to the organization's momentum.

## Aligning and Repurposing the Senior Team

The third interrelated domain is ensuring that the senior executive team has the right talent with the right skills in the right positions in order to execute the business strategy. The new CEO must ensure, from the onset, that each member of the executive team is aligned with the new leader around goals, priorities, and key business strategies.

From the selection of the new CEO, to the transfer of leadership from the outgoing to the incoming leader, to the new leader's first years in office, the transitioning of a CEO must be viewed in the context of organizational transition in order to ensure business continuity and organization success.

Our viewpoint is that the determinants of a successful CEO transition are an ongoing alignment of key constituents on strategic issues and in the confidence of key stakeholders in the new leader. Determinants of success are also marked by early accomplishments by the new leader, in the retention of key talent, and in the ability of the organization to maintain its momentum and achieve higher levels of performance. These are the measures of a successful CEO transition.

## An Opportunity to Demonstrate Strength and Resolve

The transitioning of leadership is a challenging and highly consequential moment in the life of any organization. It's an emotional period fraught with uncertainty, confusion, and for some, even fear. A time of transition is also an opportunity for a company and its leaders to demonstrate leadership, confidence, and strategic resolve, and to display the strength and conviction of the organization to achieve higher levels of performance. It is also an opportunity for the company's top leaders to restrain of personal needs for the well-being of the organization.

A board's approach to leadership transition with the emotional courage to manage the dynamics of its incoming and outgoing leaders, a genuine intent to retain the company's best talent with rewarding careers, and a well-conceived communications plan that speaks to the company's confidence and resolve, is a powerful opportunity to influence the organization in a deep and positive way.

For the outgoing CEO, the transition of leadership is an opportunity to add a final and most memorable chapter to his or her legacy by transferring knowledge with integrity and generosity of spirit and relinquishing power with grace.

For the incoming CEO, it is an opportunity to show, from the onset, a desire to listen to and learn from the organization, to build relationships with all constituents, and to build on the strategic direction and growth of the company. It is an opportunity for the new CEO and board to visibly bridge the gap between the old and the new and confidently move the company forward with renewed momentum.

# Key Insights

In our estimation, the CEO transition period encompasses the entire interval of time that begins when the board makes its final decision on who the next leader will be, includes the transfer of leadership between the outgoing and incoming CEOs, and continues on through the first two years of the new CEO's term of office.

Boards can play a strong, supportive role during the transitioning process by focusing their attention on the critical areas that are insufficiently attended to or often completely overlooked during a transition of leadership in order to ensure the uninterrupted continuity of business:

- Managing the dynamics between the outgoing and incoming CEOs to ensure a smooth and thorough transfer of knowledge and enable the new CEO to establish his or her own mark of leadership.
- Making every effort to retain top talent, especially the CEO candidates unsuccessful in their bid for the top leader position, but crucial, nevertheless, to the future success of the organization.
- Developing and releasing a well-designed, well-timed communications plan that maintains employee focus and motivation and reinforces shareholder and marketplace confidence.

Our belief is that a most important activity for a new CEO to engage in during the first three months of office is to meet all the important stakeholder groups, not as a speaker, but as the audience. His or her genuine intent must be to listen to and understand the organization through the eyes of employees, customers, suppliers, investors, and other stakeholders.

# Measure Performance and Improve Process

# 13

*"Checking the results of a decision against its expectations shows executives what their strengths are, where they need to improve, and where they lack knowledge or information."*
—Peter F. Drucker[1]

*"Those who cannot remember the past are condemned to repeat it."*
—George Santayana[2]

After the new CEO is selected and the transition from the outgoing CEO to the incoming CEO is completed, the board needs to attend to two more important tasks. The first of these is gauging how the new CEO is performing in the new role during the critical first year. The second is to conduct a review of how the CEO succession process went. The first of these tasks is critical to identify any early indicators of problems that need to be addressed early in the new CEO's term of office. The second provides the opportunity to capture lessons learned while they are still fresh and to make adjustments in the CEO succession process.

## MEASURING THE PERFORMANCE OF THE NEW CEO

The challenge for boards today is to strike a balanced, workable relationship with their CEOs—one that is both collaborative and supervisory. What complicates matters is that CEOs are purposefully hired to be self-directing, resourceful leaders who are expected to drive the agenda, not require supervision.

Moreover, although this is a reporting structure on paper, it is by no means purely supervisory. There is a peer-to-peer partnership that should be present between the board and CEO. Nevertheless, given the powerful personalities at play, the supervisory role is still a delicate responsibility to navigate and there are numerous social and psychological reasons why well-meaning, conscientious boards do not adhere to a formal evaluation process. Boards are more inclined to strike a positive relationship at the onset, not one that is potentially confrontational or makes the CEO feel as if he or she is not trusted or respected. This can lead boards to refrain from providing performance feedback during the "honeymoon" period.

What we have discovered in our transition research and interviews of CEOs is that CEOs actually want more interaction with their boards, especially during their first year in office, as long as it is not overly intrusive. CEOs feel they can benefit from the advice and support of their boards, given that board members are, by and large, experienced CEOs themselves. They also value real-time feedback about how they are performing and what they can do to improve their effectiveness.[3]

We believe the most constructive position to take is for boards and CEOs to view measuring performance as a partnership where the board and CEO come together to tackle issues and collaborate on solutions for the success of the organization. With this mindset, engaging in regular and professional reviews of expectations and performance should strengthen not strain the relationship between the board and the CEO.

## TAKING STOCK IN THE CRITICAL FIRST YEAR

The reality is that in today's complex business environment, given the importance of leadership development and succession planning, and the shortening tenures of CEOs, a purely collegial, hands-off relationship that may have marked an earlier era is no longer sufficient or recommended.

Moreover, the increasing rate of CEO failures over the past 20 years has brought far greater scrutiny from shareholders, consumer groups, and government agencies on the proper role of boards, particularly those of large, mature public companies. Directors are being pressured to take a more active role in oversight and governance and to insert themselves more into the management of the company.

In some instances, the involvement of the board as a support group is invaluable. The new CEO may be inheriting a fluid situation involving a restructuring, acquisition, or expansion that he or she will need to navigate from day one. The board may be obligated to stay very close to the situation and support the CEO's actions and decisions or even share in the deliberations until the undertaking has passed or is well under control.

Consider the crisis Brian Moynihan inherited when Bank of America's board of directors named him the successor CEO to Ken Lewis, who abruptly resigned in December 2009 in the midst of a severe recession.

In June 2008, at the onset of the worst housing slump since the 1930s, Lewis bought Countrywide Financial, the nation's biggest home lender. His intent was to rescue the company and rebuild it. And in September 2008, as financial markets neared collapse, Lewis acquired Merrill Lynch, the world's largest brokerage firm. The Merrill Lynch acquisition required Bank of America to accept $45 billion in TARP (Troubled Asset Relief Program) funds from the federal government.[4] To make matters worse, the U.S. economy shrank throughout 2009, including a 6.4 percent decline in the GDP in the first three months of Moynihan's term of office in 2010.[5]

Given the investigation of the Merrill Lynch and Countryside acquisitions by Congress, the SEC, and the New York attorney general, and the outrage expressed by employees, investors, and consumer groups, Brian Moynihan's board needed to be an intimate and highly visible partner to the CEO in all proceedings. The board's involvement was not an option; regulators and shareholders alike expected it.

As seen in this and many other examples, market and regulatory forces are compelling boards to govern at levels of detail once considered micromanagement, but are now an expectation in the current environment of heightened governance accountability, consumer activism, and shareholder demand.

So how does the board get a bead on how the new CEO is doing in year one? The CEO's assessment of his or her own performance is clearly one source, but there are other mechanisms that are useful in helping boards confirm for themselves how well the CEO is functioning.

For instance, there are enough natural touch points directly into the organization through the board's committee structure:

- Through the compensation committee's interactions with the senior HR leaders, the board can get a sense of how the organization is embracing the new leader.
- The audit committee with oversight across a range of activities including financial reporting, regulatory compliance, risk management, and ethics, can gather an early and invaluable perspective through their interactions with the CFO.
- Governance and other board committees can gauge the acceptance of the new CEO as they oversee the company's social responsibilities and public issues that affect investors and other key stakeholders, including charitable donations, political contributions, and lobbying activities.

It may be just a matter of the board keeping its finger on the pulse of the senior management team—a harbinger of the organization as a whole since the executive team is the first line of engagement with the new leader's style, vision, and temperament. Are the company's key executives engaged and energized or discouraged and departing?

Finally, the role of lead director cannot be undervalued in this first year. A lead director with sound judgment and relational skills can become the most important relationship to the CEO outside of his or her personal life. A perceptive lead director can get under the numbers to gauge the confidence and fortitude of the new CEO and become a calming, trusting force early on and throughout a CEO's tenure. This is particularly true if the outgoing CEO remains on the board. The lead director, in those instances, can provide invaluable facilitation in helping to support a constructive relationship between the former CEO and her/his successor.

## Using The Winning Formula for Measuring Performance

In addition to the board's standard dealings with company management, we believe The Winning Formula—as defined in Chapter 11—provides a very useful gauge for measuring success in the critical first year of a new CEO's term of office. The Winning Formula prioritizes the issues, opportunities, and actions that the CEO must address from the onset and over the next five to ten years and can serve as a guide for the most specific discussions as to how the new CEO is performing.

The Winning Formula first describes the operational landscape that the company will be maneuvering in over the next several years—from global economics, to shifts in technology, to the regulatory environment, to cultural and political trends.

It also profiles the requisite leadership skills and character traits of the successor CEO—the capabilities needed to strengthen the organization, engender the confidence and trust of all constituents, and ultimately deliver the strategy and business plan. The Winning Formula catalogs the essential role imperatives and requisite leadership behaviors expected of the incoming CEO—the actions and behaviors that should reveal themselves in the first year of a new CEO's term of office.

In its best sense, The Winning Formula actually serves a dual role. It is the one document that bridges CEO performance to the succession planning process by linking the new leader's effectiveness to the rationale that led the board to choose the CEO in the first place.

### IMPROVING THE SUCCESSION PLANNING PROCESS

The first year of a new CEO's term of office is also an optimal time to examine how and what decisions were made during the succession planning process and to reinforce the best procedures and correct or eliminate steps that detracted from best practice.

The idea is not to rely on the board's memory as to what happened during the last CEO succession. Details are easily forgotten in the seven to ten years of succession cycles. Moreover, the composition of the board may have changed dramatically with an influx of new board members unfamiliar with the company and culture, and inexperienced in succession planning.

## Assessing the Pros and Cons

Within the first year of a new CEO's term of office, the board should assess every step of the leadership development and succession planning process to highlight those procedures that effectively and efficiently resulted in the selection of the current CEO and are worth repeating. The board will also want to identify process problems that detracted from best practice and figure out how to correct each issue:

### Examples of steps worth repeating:

- The last CEO worked closely with the board and HR to identify a number of candidates in the first year of office, giving the company several years to thoroughly develop and assess those candidates. This is a step that the board will want to replicate with this new CEO—to identify successors early on.
- The search firm used by the board gave the company two outstanding candidates two years prior to the transition date. One became the new head of marketing, and the other, president of the Asian division. The board will want to maintain that relationship with the search firm in order to benchmark external talent and augment the next crop of CEO candidates with new recruits.
- The board used a psychological assessment firm to evaluate the candidates in order to delve beyond the tangible, visible skills into the deeper intangibles of our CEO candidates such as character and ethics. The assessment firm also developed an excellent independent view on the references provided by the outside candidates.

### Examples of areas that might be modified:

- Last time, the board insisted on a six-month overlap between the outgoing and incoming CEOs. We learned since that three months is a sufficient length of time for the transfer of knowledge. We also learned that the lead director should sit in on some of those exchanges between the outgoing and incoming CEOs to ensure that the two executives are working well together and covering all the bases.

- In this past succession, we had a special CEO selection committee oversee the succession process. While this was intended to save time for board members, it might be determined that in the future, the whole board should be more involved in the succession process. It could be decided that leadership succession in all key roles will become a standing agenda item for the entire board at every board meeting.
- The board had an emergency succession plan but when the last CEO became ill, we discovered that plan was woefully inadequate. The board will need to add greater dimension to its emergency succession plan. Having the name of an executive in an envelope is simply not enough.
- After seeing two internal succession candidates leave the company, the board might decide to be more proactive in putting together retention packages for all key executives that the company wants to retain.

## Safeguarding Business Continuity

In a broader sense, the reason for evaluating and improving the CEO succession process is not simply to improve the process of developing and appointing a successor. Though selecting the right CEO is *the* goal and certainly the ultimate criterion of success, CEO succession is not an isolated event, but rather a continuous planning and development process expressly undertaken to safeguard business continuity.

Reviewing and improving the succession planning process after each leadership transition not only ensures the selection of the best possible candidate, but also makes certain that the company emerges intact, aligned, and stronger from what is arguably its most disruptive undertaking.

In our experience, the following criteria serve as a best practice checklist of desired outcomes for boards when evaluating and improving its CEO succession process:

- The strategic plan serves as the mechanism that defines the leader profile and calibrates the development programs of internal candidates.

- An immediately effective CEO is in office with the next cycle of successors identified and in the development pipeline.
- Highly talented people are retained—even those candidates who were unsuccessful in their bid for the top position.
- An emergency succession plan is in place ensuring business continuity in the event of an unplanned departure.

## Beyond the Checklist

Boards may be doing everything right and by the book, and after every succession, take the necessary steps to improve the process and ensure the next transition runs even more smoothly. Nevertheless, directors must also be attentive to the psychological forces that sometimes defy improvement and can detract from a disciplined succession planning process, and as a result, compromise the progress, performance, and ultimate success of the incoming CEO.

- Irreconcilable differences among board members or between boards and their CEOs can result in a lack of deep strategic reflection and genuine consensus at the board level. More often than not, this leads to selecting the wrong successor for the wrong reasons.
- Domineering CEOs, in their last years of office, may have difficulty distinguishing between personal legacy and the needs of the corporation and may be reluctant to step aside when the time comes. We have noticed that this attitude is more prevalent in instances where the board did not hire the CEO—but the outgoing leader did. A successor, selected and empowered by the outgoing CEO, may believe that he or she is not fully accountable to the board, or need not be strategically aligned with the board. This can become even more untenable when the outgoing CEO remains on as the board chair.
- Individual directors often approach succession planning with a candidate in mind. Such competing agendas have the potential to compromise strategic plans and scuttle leadership development programs. A number of failed successions are the result of boards or management risking everything on one candidate who drops out within months of the transition date.

- Treating CEO succession as a dreaded, episodic event that occurs once every five to ten years instead of as an ongoing process prevents boards and management from consciously developing deep pools of executive talent—successors ready to assume leadership in the event of an unplanned departure.

These and other relational dynamics are unavoidable but must be attended to during and at the close of each succession cycle. Boards are best served by chronicling the succession process, engaging in an open and honest dialogue, and exposing all the issues that either helped or hindered the most recent transition of leadership.

The board must hold to the belief that the greater the care and discipline given to the succession process, the more successful their performance as a board, the more productive the CEO, and the more successful the organization.

---

## Key Insights

✓ The first year of office is a critical time to measure the CEO's performance against board expectations.

✓ Best practice recommends that boards conduct a review of all the succession process steps after the selection and transition of the new CEO is completed while the process is still fresh on board members' minds. This early capturing of process and procedures is critical to the continuous improvement of the succession planning process.

✓ CEOs actually want more interaction with their boards, particularly during their first year in office. CEOs feel they can benefit from the advice and support of their boards. They also value real time feedback about how they are performing and what they can do to improve their effectiveness.

✓ The most constructive attitude for boards and CEOs to adopt is to view measuring performance as a partnership where the board and new leader come together to review how things are going and to collaborate in addressing challenges for the success of the organization. Engaging in regular and professional reviews of expectations and performance should strengthen not strain the relationship between the board and the CEO.

✓ The CEO's assessment of and confidence in his or her own performance is clearly one early indicator for determining how well the
new leader is doing in the first year of office. But there are other
mechanisms that are useful in helping boards confirm for themselves
how well the CEO is performing, primarily senior management relations through the board's committee structure.

✓ A lead director with sound judgment and relational skills can become
the most important relationship broker for the CEO. A perceptive
lead director can get under the numbers to gauge the confidence and
fortitude of the new CEO and become a calming, trusting force early
on and throughout a CEO's tenure.

✓ Reviewing and improving the succession planning process after each
leadership transition not only ensures the selection of the best possible candidate, but also makes certain that the company emerges
intact, aligned, and stronger from what is arguably its most disruptive undertaking.

# MANAGE THE DYNAMICS IN CEO SUCCESSION

# 14

*"Coming together is a beginning; keeping together is progress; working together is success."*

—Henry Ford[1]

While each of the previous nine dimensions to effective CEO succession planning defines a specific stage in the succession process with identifiable tasks and outcomes, this tenth and final dimension addresses the relational dynamics among the various players involved in each stage of the process.

This tenth dimension speaks to the personal emotions and challenges that have a direct bearing on the thoughts and actions of the executives involved, affecting how they view themselves and their relationship with their peers and superiors. These driving, often conflicting forces of ego, position power, fear, financial motivations and uncertainty seldom rise above the surface in business. Yet they add a layer of complexity when left unresolved or only shared in private with a spouse, close friend, or mentor.

Our point of view is that boards and CEOs can be far more productive and successful if these emotions and motivations are openly acknowledged and resolved. How individuals feel about themselves directly impacts how they engage with others, and allowing personal issues to fester may eventually erode the relationship between board and management and weaken a company's momentum and success.

By effectively managing the personal feelings that will always well up during succession planning, stakeholders can channel their experiences, and energy into a powerful, productive force for the benefit of the organization and ultimately themselves.

When we review the pattern of relational dynamics present in CEO succession, our nine dimensions unite under three essential themes that cover the full spectrum of succession planning. They are reflected here as goal statements—a model of partnership and best practice:

### Partner in all aspects of succession planning

- Establish board ownership, involvement, and oversight
- Set succession time frames
- Align on strategy and purpose

### Cultivate the talent, skills, and character of your high potentials

- Prepare for emergencies
- Build the talent pipeline
- Source external talent and manage search firms

### Safeguard the transfer and assent of leadership

- Select the CEO
- Proactively manage the transition
- Measure performance and improve the process

This model of partnership requires that boards and senior management reach outside of themselves in order to unite with their peers and work toward a greater purpose. To understand and endure the tendencies of others, executives must first come to terms with their own emotions, needs, and expectations. Bringing this level of personal resolve, authenticity, and integrity to the table is the only way to remain centered and committed to a best possible outcome when challenges arise during the succession planning process.

## Partner in All Aspects of Succession Planning

There is hardly a board member today who doesn't understand and accept the responsibility for succession planning. Directors get it, but despite their awareness, there still exists a lack of knowledge and a wide variation of skills, comfort, and experience with the process.

We have always believed that a board of directors should be *the* governing body entrusted with full accountability for CEO succession planning, yet the real current of understanding runs much deeper than simply acknowledging who owns succession planning and why. There must be an authentic partnership between the board and CEO to make the process truly work.

CEOs, though, are generally ambivalent about engaging in succession planning. In the beginning stages of tenure, the CEO's focus is appropriately on the business-at-hand, driving his or her strategic agenda, aligning with the board, and developing a working relationship with the senior team. CEOs are not thinking about the end of their tenure, but rather the demands and challenges of the here and now.

CEOs may also feel that bringing up the issue of succession may signal to the board a loss of confidence, change of heart, or lack of loyalty to the company. The CEO may also feel that their end date is of their own choosing, a date in the future that they will determine at a time that suits their personal needs and sense of accomplishment.

Directors are also hesitant about discussing succession processes and time frames. Bringing up the issue of the transfer of leadership early in a CEO's tenure may imply a lack of confidence in the new leader, provoking feelings of inadequacy and potentially prompting an unplanned departure if not handled tactfully. Board members may also be afraid of compromising their relationship with the CEO, who may have invited them to serve on the board in the first place.

For these reasons, most CEOs and boards tend to defer thinking about succession until a transition date is imminent—usually within 12 to 18 months of the CEO's retirement. But to approach succession planning as a best practice, it's crucial that a realistic time frame be established early on to ensure the thorough development of internal candidates and mitigate the need to parachute in an outsider in the event of an unplanned departure.

The key insight is instilling a higher level of awareness in the sitting CEO by redirecting his or her attention away from personal gain toward the needs of the organization. A conscientious board chair or independent director should have a candid conversation regarding time frames with the CEO-as-candidate during the interview process or as early as possible in the new leader's term of office. If approached as a matter of course, the discussion of an end date is not interpreted as a vote of no confidence, but rather the genuine interest on the part of the board to ensure business continuity.

## Cultivate the Talent, Skills, and Character of Your High Potentials

An absence of leadership in today's marketplace—for any period—is a dangerous and risky way to run a business. A company without a CEO at the helm is exposed and at its most vulnerable—a situation that can directly affect employee morale and productivity, market position, and share value.

Boards compound emergency succession crises by not being prepared. Out of fear of loss of momentum, investor confidence, and share value, boards caught off-guard will invariably make emotional and tactical errors in judgment as they scramble to gain control over an unraveling situation.

Directors must be ready to contend with an unexpected change of leadership—at any level in the organization and for any reason. They must react quickly, but with calmness and decisiveness. They must assure employees, customers, and investors that new leadership will soon be in place, that the company has a strong footing, that employees are motivated, and that the business will continue to move forward.

Being prepared for an emergency is one thing, but minimizing or even eliminating the cause for emergencies is quite another. Continuous leadership development, better vetting of external talent, and having a lead director or non-executive chair maintain a trusting, confiding relationship with the sitting CEO all help minimize if not eliminate the possibility of an unplanned succession.

Companies that are able to sustain their success have CEOs and boards actively involved in the cultivation and advancement of internal talent. They maintain highly effective CEO succession-planning programs that succeed in attracting and retaining valuable talent well in advance of the CEO's transition date, and they accelerate the development of their high-potentials with stretch assignments that hone future-leaning talents and skills.

Yet, there are challenges that prevent CEOs from identifying succession candidates early on and letting those chosen ones know that they are in consideration. Such discussions could distract key players from pressing business issues, potentially create horse races among contenders, and emotionally disrupt an otherwise-stable working relationship among the senior team.

Furthermore, CEOs and HR executives will need to wrestle with how to tell valued executives that they are not potential successors and why. These difficult conversations are often postponed or avoided out of fear of demotivating and potentially losing key talent long before a CEO's term of office ends.

Another best practice in succession planning that creates additional stress points for the CEO is availing successor candidates the opportunity to interact with the board. The unstructured exposure of a CEO's direct reports with his or her bosses can render the top leader vulnerable as candidates may inadvertently, or even purposefully, divulge something that may embarrass or compromise the CEO.

The best practice is for the CEO and senior HR leader to engage in discussions with all direct reports on their strengths, weaknesses, and aspirations before selecting successors. This is where the CEO needs to take the lead. If someone aspires to succeed the CEO and the top leader doesn't believe the aspirant has the right stuff, then the CEO needs to have a forthright but supportive discussion with that individual so as not to lose someone whose talents can be directed toward an equally satisfying career within the organization.

## Safeguard the Transfer and Assent of Leadership

The most important decision any board of directors can make is the selection of the CEO. Getting this decision right can have significant impact on the trajectory and sustained success of an organization, while getting it wrong can set in motion a ripple effect of adverse consequences that can detract from positive growth and even destroy a legacy of business success.

Since the board must live with their choice of successor for years to follow, they owe it to themselves and their shareholders to invest the upfront time to gain a deeper understanding of each individual candidate. While a potential successor's business acumen is relatively easy to gauge in formal settings, directors most often feel inadequate when it comes to assessing the ethics and integrity of an executive. Informal, unstructured meetings where candidates can let their hair down and reveal their true character and personality will help board members get to know the person behind the promotional facade.

Once the new CEO is chosen, the work of the board is far from over as the dynamic shifts to the transfer of leadership. Though a challenging and highly emotional period filled with uncertainty and confusion, the transitioning of leadership is an opportunity for the board and senior management to demonstrate leadership, confidence, and strategic resolve; and for the outgoing CEO to model the restraint of personal needs for the well-being of the organization.

The central goal in transitioning leadership is ensuring that the transfer of knowledge, responsibilities, and relationships are accomplished without interrupting the focus and momentum of the organization. The challenge is in navigating the personal emotions of the incoming and outgoing CEOs, as well as the relational dynamics between both executives that can impede the process and disrupt an otherwise smooth transition.

The outgoing CEO may be experiencing the fear of loss of power or may feel unappreciated for all that was accomplished during his or her administration. This can create reluctance on the part of the outgoing leader to let go of power and even delay the transfer of authority.

The incoming CEO may overestimate his or her own skills or underestimate the scope and complexity of the job and attempt to do too much too quickly. Then there are those who are immediately seduced by the power of the position—inducements that can transform personalities, inflate egos, or weaken a leader's integrity and purpose.

There are also the interpersonal dynamics between the outgoing and incoming CEOs; the outgoing CEO may feel as if the incoming leader is trying to change things too quickly; and the incoming CEO may feel that the departing CEO is unwilling to relinquish power.

To ensure a successful transition of leadership, these powerful psychological dynamics require attentive and unwavering oversight, wisdom, and judgment on the part of an attentive lead director or non-executive chair who is prepared to mediate and advance the interactions between the outgoing and incoming CEOs.

## THE UPWARD SPIRAL OF SUCCESSION

The word "succession" in itself is a positive term—a chronological sequence of events that are not lateral but ascending. Succession should epitomize an upward spiral of continual improvement and growth.

This, to us, is the deeper meaning of CEO succession planning: every cycle of leadership spirals the company upward, enabling each new leader to stand on the shoulders of his or her predecessor and expand the growth of the organization.

CEO succession is far more than the transitioning of a company's leadership; it is a process fundamental to the sustained success of a company. The only path to this successful outcome is for boards and CEOs to manage their personal issues, focus on a higher goal, and authentically work together in all aspects of CEO succession planning—from aligning on strategy and purpose, to continuously cultivating a talent pipeline of leaders for all levels of the organization, to facilitating an effortless transition of leadership.

---

### Key Insights

✓ Beyond the relational dynamics among the various players involved in each stage of the succession planning process, personal challenges, motivations and emotions can have a direct bearing on the thoughts and actions of the executives involved.

✓ How individuals feel about themselves directly affects how they engage with others, and by allowing personal emotions to fester may eventually erode the relationship between board and management and weaken a company's momentum and success.

✓ To understand and endure the tendencies of others, executives must first come to terms with their own emotions, needs, motivations and expectations. Bringing this level of personal resolve, authenticity, and integrity to the table is the only way to remain centered and committed to a best possible outcome when challenges arise during the succession-planning process.

# Epilogue: Perspectives on the Future

Reflecting back across our years of practice in supporting boards and CEOs in their succession planning efforts, and observing today, as we help companies assess and prepare for future successions, we have recognized developing trends that we believe will notably influence talent development and succession planning in the years to come.

Every year ushers in new and unpredictable issues and opportunities, but these trends are what we believe to be the transformational movements—developments that will contextually affect how boards and CEOs approach and plan for CEO succession in the next ten years and beyond.

## Five Perspectives on the Future of CEO Succession Planning

- The Accelerating Need for Knowledge Retention and Sharing
- The Nature and Role of the Twenty-First Century CEO
- Systematizing the Transition of Leadership
- The Pursuit of Gender Balance for Competitive Advantage
- The Cultural Rotation of Top Leadership

## The Accelerating Need for Knowledge Retention and Sharing

The war for talent will become the war for knowledge, a resource battle that will heat up over the next ten years as the rate of retiring baby boomers accelerates—and not just in the United States, but in all developed nations. In 2006, the leading edge of the baby boomer generation reached 60 years of age across the globe. In the United States in 2012, 80 million boomers will retire with an additional three to four million retiring every year through 2030.[1]

The leadership pool of executives (ages 35 to 50), which grew 3 to 4 percent over the last four decades of the twentieth century, has declined by 2 to 3 percent in the first decade of this century. By 2020, estimates are that the *Fortune* 500 will face a turnover of about half of its workforce with an even higher rate of turnover in senior management and board-level positions.[2]

In a knowledge economy, company- and industry-specific information and insight will become increasingly critical to the sustainability, performance, and innovation of every company. As corporate leaders retire, with them departs cultivated skills and experience, historical context of corporate culture and strategic vision, business wisdom, interpersonal relationships, and external networks—all receding at an unprecedented rate.

Given the accelerating rate of retirement, the capture and transfer of knowledge from outgoing leader to incoming leader will be indispensable to an organization's business continuity and competitive advantage. Yet, according to a recent report from The Conference Board, most companies do not have a plan to manage and transfer knowledge and even fewer factor cross-generational challenges into their business strategy.[3]

### Implications for Succession Planning

- Accelerating rates of retirement will require an ongoing effort to grow talent from within the organization in order to build on and retain historical context and strategic vision.
- Organizations must create pools of candidates with high leadership potential and proactively provide opportunities for them to reach their developmental goals. Success in succession relies on flexibility in recruiting and developing future talent.
- Every effort must be made to retain unsuccessful succession candidates and other key talent—at all levels of the organization—in order to retain their talents and skills and preserve their organizational and cultural knowledge.

## The Nature and Role of the Twenty-First Century CEO

It is very difficult for companies to escape the mindset of the twentieth century and the quest for the hero leader. But as we venture further into the twenty-first century, the focus of boards and senior management will necessarily shift from hiring CEOs who lead with position power to those who lead by encouraging ideas—from acting as the iconic, external voice of the company to being the uniting, enabling voice behind all talent.

Multinational companies today face business opportunities and challenges that are deeply complex and interconnected. These organizations are comprised of thousands of employees in dozens of countries with varying cultural and political differences, and with variations in their work ethic, reporting structures, and goals. No one leader can possibly hold all the answers to all the problems, challenges, and opportunities facing such vast organizations.

The past, heroic approach to leadership will yield to an ensemble leadership style over the next decade and become the dominant trait of the global leader in the years to come. The responsibilities that were once the domain of an individual CEO will disperse to other stewards in the enterprise and in other regions of the world. The twenty-first century CEO will become more of an integrator of knowledge than the single source of knowledge, wisdom, and decision.

The CEO's role in the future will be to empower the senior team and spread that empowerment deep within and across the organization to those on the front line who directly influence and drive change. The CEO of the future will no longer be a singularly powerful individual prone to making decisions in isolation. He or she will be a team player, willing to collaborate, and obsessed with enabling value through others.

## Implications for Succession Planning

- This emphasizes the need to develop leaders from within the organization, individuals who are intimately familiar with the company's culture, capabilities, and processes.
- Candidates in development will benefit from stretch assignments in different parts of the world and in different divisions of the organization to become familiar with the companies diverse resources and opportunities.
- The character traits of the effective leader will shift from independent to interdependent, from risk to restraint, from task-driven to relationship-driven, and from sole to eclectic decision maker.

## Systematizing the Transition of Leadership

Shorter tenures for CEOs will become standard and compensation schemes for CEOs will change in response to regulatory and market pressures. Given the shorter terms, it will become more difficult to measure the progress and impact of a CEO and more critical to systematize the process of transitioning knowledge from one leader to the next and effectively accelerating and supporting the integration of the new CEO as he or she assumes office.

A CEO's tenure, on a global average, is now 7.6 years, down from 9.5 years in 1995, and in the past two decades, 30 percent of *Fortune* 500 CEOs have lasted fewer than three years in office.[4] Other studies indicate that since 2007, 40 percent of CEOs were dismissed or forced to resign within their first 18 months on the job.[5]

One of the reasons for this trend is the changing nature of the board of directors. Boards are under pressure to be more active in all manner of corporate affairs, at the same time that they are being held to a higher standard of accountability by shareholders. Since the Enron collapse in 2001, there has been a demand for greater board governance evidenced in reforms such as the Sarbanes-Oxley Act of 2002 and the SEC's 2009 rulings on CEO succession planning. Under this scrutiny, boards are much less tolerant than they were just 10 years ago, increasingly more independent of management, and more likely to take action in event of a problem.

A shorter CEO tenure need not have a negative impact on the business continuity of an organization. What boards must do is systematize the transitioning of leadership from the outgoing to the incoming CEO. Shortening tenures gives less time for a new leader to achieve results, so boards must also accelerate the integration of the new CEO in order to advance his or her effectiveness in the first year of office. Preceding all of this will be the need to have successor candidates in ready development and aligned to a dynamic, ongoing strategic plan.

### Implications for Succession Planning

- Greater attention must be given to developing leaders from within the organization—a pool of ready candidates who are intimately familiar with the company's culture, capabilities, and processes.

Every effort must then be made to retain top talent, especially CEO candidates, unsuccessful in their bid for the top leader position, but crucial, nevertheless, to the future success of the organization.

- Systematizing the transition of leadership will require greater discipline in managing the dynamics between the outgoing and incoming CEOs to ensure a smooth and thorough transfer of knowledge. This could include the participation of a lead director who can facilitate and ensure the smooth and thorough transfer of knowledge.
- Systematizing the transition of leadership will also require accelerating the integration of the new CEO within the first three to twelve months to maintain organizational momentum, establish critical relationships with key stakeholders, and achieve clarity on the strategic priorities of the organization.

## The Pursuit of Gender Balance for Competitive Advantage

Since the early 1980s, women have surpassed men in attaining both undergraduate and post-graduate degrees; they have controlled or influenced over 80 percent of all consumer-spending decisions; and they have occupied over 50 percent of the middle management positions in *Fortune* 500 companies.[6]

It would be consistent then that over the course of these past three decades, women would be at or near an equal level with men in career opportunity and advancement. Although there has been equal numbers of men and women in the labor force since the 1980s, the reality is that over the course of the past 30 years, women have done no better than to secure 15 percent of senior management positions, less than 15 percent of board-level positions, and less than 3 percent of CEO positions. In 2010, only 15 percent of senior executives were women, an insignificant change from 14 percent in 1996. And in 2010, less than 3 percent of CEOs were women, with no change since 1996.[7]

This sluggish improvement in balanced gender representation on boards and in executive ranks persists in the face of numerous studies that show that companies that are inclusive of both women and men at all management levels make better decisions, are more productive, more innovative, more attentive to diverse customer groups, and realize better financial results than companies that are less diverse.[8]

The percent of women as senior executives, CEOs, and board members will not significantly change in the next ten years but there are dynamics in the marketplace that will cause the percentage of women in senior leadership roles to increase at a faster rate.

When considering the global war for talent and the growing need for global leadership skills that are more inclusive and participative in decision making, companies may increase their consideration of women for leadership positions. This will not develop out of a sense of fairness and equality—the rationale of the past 40 years—but more from the standpoint of the economic advantage gained through the availability of internal talent pools, the collaborative nature of women leaders, and the expectations of an increasingly gender diverse marketplace.

### Implications for Succession Planning

- Recruitment programs targeted at women for senior level positions will secure skilled executives from organizations that fail to promote its women leaders.
- Recruitment is only half the solution. Companies must make every effort to retain their skilled leadership through executive mentoring and merit-based leadership development programs.
- More attention and intelligence must be given to the distinct leadership skills of women and men, as successor candidates are given situational leadership assignments that accentuate and develop those unique skills.

## The Cultural Rotation of Top Leadership

The most important force shaping global business today is the demand from emerging markets, as the economic growth of developing nations is already outpacing the developed world. While 65 percent of the world's GDP is currently produced in developed countries and 35 percent in emerging countries, current estimates suggest that over the course of the next 10 to 20 years, that statistic will invert as two-thirds of the world's GDP will come from emerging markets such as China, India, South Korea, Brazil, and Russia.[9]

The implications of this shift will have a transformational effect on leadership development and succession planning for global companies. Leadership and management styles differ across cultures and the selection of CEOs who represent the source of growth and reflect the cultural mosaic that is becoming the mainstay of many global organizations will increasingly become a key criterion for succession for multinational companies—even for companies whose headquarters are in the United States.

CEOs who understand, appreciate, and motivate employees across multiple cultures will become an increasingly valued resource. Future leaders will need to be seen as citizens of the world with an expanded field of vision and values.

CEOs will also need to appreciate cultural diversity. They will need to understand the social and motivational differences that influence how and why employees of the same global company work differently in various countries. A global CEO who resembles and comprehends other cultures will not just be good optics—he or she will be the key to competing successfully in developing nations in the future.

## Implications for Succession Planning

- Identifying successor candidates will need to become a global succession planning effort with candidates nominated from various regions of the world.
- Two- to three-year stretch assignments will require a rotation of candidates from various countries so CEO successors will gain better visibility for business practices and resources with cultures.
- The talents and skills of global CEOs will expand beyond business and financial acumen to include such skills as language fluency, world history, economics, and socio-cultural dynamics.

# APPENDIX: TEN QUESTIONS A DIRECTOR SHOULD ASK

Here is a series of questions a responsible director should ask to ensure that a board of directors is cultivating a best practice in its most important area of governance—CEO succession planning. These questions align with our 10 Key Dimensions of effective CEO succession planning and our commentary offers a guide as to what a director should hope to hear as confirmation of a best practice.

In virtually every instance, the director should anticipate the involvement of a lead director, orchestrating the way in which board ownership for CEO succession planning is defined and managed—in partnership with the CEO.

An independent lead director with sound judgment and relational skills can become the most important relationship broker among board members and between the board and CEO. A perceptive lead director can be a neutral, calming voice of reason during emotionally challenging moments and a mentor and coach early on and throughout a CEO's tenure.

## 1. Is Our Board Taking Primary Responsibility for CEO Succession Planning?

The board of directors should be *the* governing body entrusted with full accountability for CEO succession planning, though the real current of understanding must run more deeply than simply acknowledging who owns it and why.

Although the board is accountable for the process, there must be a partnership between board and CEO—a partnership built on authenticity and trust. The board and CEO should have an understanding of involvement—a division of labor orchestrated by the board and adhered to by both parties.

## 2. Does Our Board Have an Adequate Succession Planning Time Frame that Allows for Candidate Development and Leadership Transition?

Given the complexity of the role of the CEO, comprehensive preparation of internal candidates should begin at least five years in advance of an anticipated transition. CEO succession planning should begin immediately following the instatement of a new CEO and be a constant, ongoing process managed as closely and attentively as any of the company's critical business issues.

## 3. What Is the Emergency CEO Succession Plan?

The key insight is not just being prepared for emergency successions, but significantly reducing or even eliminating the causes through pre-planning. A good emergency plan goes beyond just having the name of an interim or replacement successor.

An emergency succession plan requires a communications plan prepared in advance, interim leadership staffing and decision-making, and a host of activities both inside and outside the firm that should be reviewed and updated annually. There are also interrelated moves within the organization that must be thought through and updated on an ongoing basis, as key players are constantly moving up, laterally, or out as a result of performance and opportunity.

## 4. Is Our Board Aligned on the Company's Vision and Strategic Direction, and Does that Strategic Plan Define the Talents and Skills Required of the CEO?

Defining the strategic direction of the company, in partnership with the incumbent CEO, and the leadership skills required to advance the organization into that future are arguably the most fundamental responsibilities of a board. The board's alignment of these two necessarily linked decisions ultimately determines the future direction of the company and the successor most capable of leading. The Leader Profile should be a living document, reviewed at least annually to reflect any changes made to the strategic plan, to lend direction to candidate development, and to confirm the ongoing capabilities of the sitting CEO.

## 5. Does Our Company Have a Rigorous Talent Development Program?

Board and management must, together, promote a culture of learning and development to attract and retain valuable, and in some instances, premium talent. They must be dedicated to creating leadership development programs that accelerate the development of their high-potential candidates.

The leadership development programs should not only develop the strategic and operational skills and abilities of its future leaders, but also be designed to shape their character traits of emotional intelligence, integrity, sound judgment, courage, and humility.

## 6. What Is Our Company's External Talent Assessment Process?

The best way to ensure that a company's leadership development and succession planning program is dynamic and future leaning is to cultivate internal candidates who are not only the best and brightest within the company—but also the best and brightest in the industry.

This requires benchmarking the skills and accomplishments of external talent during the succession planning process and using the intelligence gathered to augment internal training and development programs and even recruit outside talent early on in the process.

## 7. What Is Our Board's Vetting Process for the Final Selection of the New CEO?

Selecting the CEO is a board-level decision. Because of the significant value afforded a company when making the right decision, and the immeasurable cost for getting it wrong, the CEO selection decision must be grounded in a thorough and in-depth assessment of both the hard/technical requirements of the position and the "softer" but equally important leadership and character requirements of each candidate.

The foundational guide for the board in this entire assessment process is the Leader Profile, the blueprint that defines the requisite leadership skills and character traits expected of the successor CEO based on the strategic plan. Additionally, the board must invest sufficient time to get to know final candidates themselves since it will have to live with its succession choice. Since the full board will live with their selection decision, the vetting process of final candidates should involve all board members to some extent, even if a board committee assumes primary responsibility to oversee the process.

### 8. What Procedures Are in Place for Transitioning the CEO Position—From Transfer of Leadership to Integration of the New CEO?

Boards that properly play a strong, supportive role during the transitioning process focus their attention on the critical areas that are sometimes overlooked during a transition of leadership, including managing the dynamics between the outgoing and incoming CEOs and making every effort to retain top talent.

Moreover, boards should not assume that the standard honeymoon period of 90 days is a sufficient amount of time for a new CEO to acclimate and begin to show results. Directors must be prepared to support the new leader, especially if the company is challenged with organizational, market, environmental, or political dynamics with focused attention for the first year at a minimum.

### 9. What Are the Board's Metrics and Milestones for Measuring the Performance of the New CEO and Improving the Succession Planning Process?

Boards and CEOs should view measuring performance as a partnership where the board and CEO come together to tackle issues and collaborate on solutions for the success of the organization. With this mindset, engaging in regular and professional reviews of expectations and performance should strengthen, not strain, the relationship between the board and the CEO.

Within the first year of a new CEO's term of office, the board should review and assess every step of the leadership development and succession planning process to highlight those procedures that effectively and efficiently resulted in the selection of the current CEO and are worth repeating. The board will also want to identify process problems that detracted from best practice and figure out how to correct each issue.

## 10. How Genuinely Open and Attentive Is the Board in Managing the Relational Dynamics and Personal Emotions Associated with the CEO Succession Process?

The only path to a successful succession outcome is for boards and CEOs to openly and authentically work together in all aspects of CEO succession planning—from aligning on strategy and purpose, to continuously cultivating a talent pipeline of leaders for all levels of the organization, to facilitating an effortless transition of leadership.

Boards and CEOs can be far more productive and successful if personal agendas and emotions are openly acknowledged and resolved. By effectively managing the personal feelings that will always well up during succession planning, directors and senior management can channel their experiences and energy into a powerful, productive force for the benefit of the organization and ultimately themselves.

RHR International is a world leader in the field of executive and organizational development. Our management psychologists and consultants work closely with C-suite leaders to accelerate individual, team and business performance. We focus on four key areas of client need—Individual Assessment, Executive Development, Senior Team Effectiveness, and CEO Succession.

## Individual Assessment

RHR International uses proven methodologies developed through decades of shared experience and state of the art research to address the considerable risks associated with leadership selection and promotion decisions. RHR also provides sophisticated, rapid and accurate assessment of management teams for acquirers and inbound CEOs.

## Executive Development

RHR International architects high-impact development experiences to engage leaders, accelerate executive integration (onboarding), improve performance through individual coaching, and increase the readiness of high potential talent for senior management roles.

## Senior Team Effectiveness

RHR International consultants work with CEOs and their top executives to help create an identity as a team, increase pace of change and align performance with reward. The result: a cohesive group of senior executives strongly aligned with the CEO's agenda and focused on achieving team performance.

## CEO Succession

RHR International helps boards, CEOs and new leaders navigate the complex and challenging process of leadership transition. Change at the top is never easy. RHR helps clients put the right process in place, and then works shoulder-to-shoulder with them to execute it.

In 1945, RHR's founders pioneered the field of executive assessment. Since that time, we have been proven difference-makers—unique in our combination of top management focus, psychologists' perspective and high-level business acumen. RHR creates client value by helping executives accelerate change, increase leadership capacity and impact, and mitigate hiring and acquisition risks.

RHR International has offices in Belgium, Brazil, Canada, China, France, Germany, Italy, Switzerland, the United Kingdom, and the United States. The company is headquartered in Chicago, IL. For more information, please visit www.rhrinternational.com or follow us on the RHR blog site (tinyurl.com/rhrblogsite), Facebook (www.facebook.com/pages/RHR-International/233669970027168), or Twitter (twitter.com/RHRIntlLLP).

# References

## Chapter One

1. CEO Succession: Has Grooming Talent on the Inside Gone by the Wayside?, Dr. Michael Useem, Knowledge@Wharton, November 28, 2007, <http://knowledge.wharton.upenn.edu/article.cfm?articleid=1845>.
2. Peter Capelli, *Talent on Demand* (Boston: Harvard Business Press, 2008)
3. Jean M. Twenge and Stacy M. Campbell, "Generational Differences in Psychological Traits and Their Impact on the Workplace," *Journal of Managerial Psychology,* 23, no. 8 (April 2012): 862–877.
4. CEO Succession: Has Grooming Talent on the Inside Gone by the Wayside?, Dr. Michael Useem, Knowledge@Wharton, November 28, 2007, <http://knowledge.wharton.upenn.edu/article.cfm?articleid=1845>.
5. Benjamin Gilad, *Business Blind Spots: Replacing Your Company's Entrenched and Outdated Myths, Beliefs and Assumptions With the Realities of Today's Markets,* (Chicago: Probus Professional Pub, 1993).
6. Kenneth A. Borokhovich, Robert Parrino, Teresa Trapani, "Outside Directors and CEO Selection." *Journal of Financial and Qualitative Analysis* 31, no. 3 (September 1996): 337–335.
7. William B. Werther Jr., "Continuity Planning as a Dimension of Corporate Governance." *Human Resource Planning* 18, no. 4 (1995).
8. James M. Citrin and Dayton Ogden, "Succeeding at Succession." *Harvard Business Review,* November 2010, 29–31.
9. Edward Ferris and Justus O'Brien, *Examining the Impact of SEC Guidance Changes on CEO Succession Planning* (New York: The Conference Board, 2010).
10. Clarke Murphy, "CEO Succession: The Ultimate Measure Of Board Performance," *The Corporate Board,* July/August 2010.

## Chapter Two

1. U.S. Securities & Exchange Commission, *Staff Legal Bulletin* No. 14E (October 2009).
2. Booz Allen Hamilton, *CEO Succession Survey 2010.*
3. Ram Charan, "Ending the CEO Succession Crisis," *Harvard Business Review,* February 2005, 72.
4. Booz Allen Hamilton, *CEO Succession Survey 2010.*
5. Warren Buffett, *2001 Chairman's Letter* (Omaha: Berkshire Hathaway, 2001).
6. Booz Allen Hamilton, *CEO Succession Survey 2010.*
7. Cari Tuna," Theory and Practice: Hiring a CEO from the Outside is More Expensive," *Wall Street Journal,* July 28, 2008, p. B5.

8. Jacqueline Doherty, "CEO Robert Selander Gets Top Marks for Making MasterCard No. 1," *Barron's 500,* May 2009.
9. McCormick & Co. Announces Q2 2011 Financials, Perfumer & Flavorist, July 1, 2011 <http://www.perfumerflavorist.com/networking/news/company/124895534.html>.
10. Robert Lawless, interviewed by RHR International, 2009.
11. "Akers, the Last Emperor," *Businessweek,* June 1991.
12. Vito J. Racanelli, "World's Most Respected Companies," *Barron's,* February 2010.
13. Mina Kimes, "Johnson & Johnson CEO Bill Weldon's Painful Year," *CNN Money,* September 7, 2010, <http://money.cnn.com/2010/09/06/news/companies/J_and_J_Bill_Weldon_Bad_Year.fortune/index.htm>.
14. Ciel S. Cantoria, "J&J Embarks on Two-Pronged Succession Planning Program," *Financial Express* September 27, 2002.
15. Deborah Jacobs, *How McDonald's Plans Ahead,* (Los Angeles: Korn/Ferry Briefings on Talent Leadership, 2011).
16. Scott Reeves, "Fiorina Is Out At HP," Forbes, 9 February 2005, <http://www.forbes.com/2005/02/09/cx_sr_0208carly.html>.
17. Eleanor Bloxham, HP's Next Act," *CNNMoney,* August 10, 2010, <http://money.cnn.com/2010/08/10/technology/HP_post_Hurd_board.fortune/index.htm>.
18. Sidney Finkelstein, "Why Ken Lewis Destroyed Bank Of America," *Forbes,* March 3, 2009.
19. David Gaffen, "How the Mighty Banks Have Fallen," *Wall Street Journal,* February 20, 2009).
20. Joann S. Lubin, "Newell Rubbermaid CEO to Step Down," *Wall Street Journal,* January 11, 2011.
21. "Phil Condit: Boeing," *Businessweek Online,* (January 12, 2004).
22. Nicole Gaudiano, "Ban on Three Boeing Rocket-Launching Companies Lifted," *AirForceTimes,* March 4, 2005.
23. Nathan Hodge, "Boeing Bid Beats Europe for Tanker," *Wall Street Journal,* February 25, 2011.
24. Ford Motor Company, *2009 Annual Report.*

## Chapter Three

1. RHR/*Directorship* joint surveys of 266 board directors (2004), and 120 directors (2005).
2. RHR/*Chief Executive* joint survey of 236 board directors (2009).
3. RHR's series of in-depth interviews with 41 board directors (2009).
4. RHR/*Chief Executive* joint survey of directors (May/June 2009).
5. Mark Nadler, Steve Krupp and Richard Hossack, "Overcoming the Obstacles to CEO Succession Planning," *Oliver Wyman Journal,* March/April 2008.
6. Booz Allen Hamilton, *CEO Succession Survey 2010.*
7. Douglas Conant, interviewed by RHR, 2009.
8. James Balloun, interviewed by RHR, 2009.
9. James Hackett, interviewed by RHR, 2009.

10. Ajay Banga, interviewed by RHR, 2009.
11. Mark Jennings, interviewed by RHR, 2009.
12. John Hanson, interviewed by RHR, 2009.
13. Manly Molpus, interviewed by RHR, 2009.
14. Leo Mullin, interviewed by RHR, 2009.
15. Raymond Viault, interviewed by RHR, 2009.

## Chapter Four

1. John C. Maxwell, *The 21 Irrefutable Laws of Leadership* (Nashville: Thomas Nelson Publishers, 1998).
2. U.S. Securities & Exchange Commission, *Staff Legal Bulletin* No. 14E (October 2009).
3. RHR/*Chief Executive* joint survey of 236 board directors (2009).
4. RHR/*Chief Executive* joint survey of 236 board directors (2009).
5. RHR/*Chief Executive* joint survey of 236 board directors (2009).
6. Booz Allen Hamilton, *CEO Succession Survey 2010.*
7. RHR/*Chief Executive* joint survey of 236 board directors (2009).
8. RHR/*Chief Executive* joint survey of 236 board directors (2009).
9. Booz Allen Hamilton, *CEO Succession Survey 2010.*
10. James M. Citrin and Dayton Ogden, "Succeeding at Succession," *Harvard Business Review,* November 2010, 29–31.

## Chapter Five

1. Quotation by John Emerich Edward Dalberg Acton, first Baron Acton (1834–1902). The historian and moralist, who was otherwise known simply as Lord Acton, expressed this opinion in a letter to Bishop Mandell Creighton in 1887.
2. Chair and CEO of a *Fortune* 500 company, interviewed by RHR, 2010.
3. RHR/*Chief Executive* joint survey of 236 board directors (2009).
4. Donald James, interviewed by RHR, 2009.
5. Peter Fasolo, interviewed by RHR, 2009.
6. U.S. Securities & Exchange Commission, *Staff Legal Bulletin* No. 14E (October 2009).
7. Reuters, "CEO Succession Planning, Powered by Apple," *Business Law Currents,* September 1, 2011.
8. Reuters, "CEO Succession Planning, Powered by Apple," *Business Law Currents* September 1, 2011.

## Chapter Six

1. RHR/*Chief Executive* joint survey of 236 board directors (2009).
2. Booz Allen Hamilton, *CEO Succession Survey 2010.*
3. James M. Citrin and Dayton Ogden, "Succeeding at Succession," *Harvard Business Review,* November 2010, 29–31.
4. John Hanson, interviewed by RHR, 2009.

5. "Ford Names New CEO," *CNNMoney*, September 5, 2006, <http://money.cnn.com/2006/09/05/news/companies/ford/index.htm>.
6. John Keller and Dennis Carey, *When Finding the Right CEO is Job #1* (Los Angeles: Korn/Ferry Institute Briefings on Talent Leadership, 2011). <http://www.kornferryinstitute.com/briefings-magazine/winter-2011/when-finding-right-ceo-job-1>.
7. John Keller, and Dennis Carey, *When Finding the Right CEO is Job #1* (Los Angeles: Korn/Ferry Institute Briefings on Talent Leadership, 2011). <http://www.kornferryinstitute.com/briefings-magazine/winter-2011/when-finding-right-ceo-job-1>.
8. Douglas Conant, interviewed by RHR, 2009.
9. Stephen Patrick, interviewed by RHR, 2009.

## Chapter Seven

1. Chief Executive, CEO Briefing Newsletter, 2011.
2. Pallavi Gogoi, "CEO Succession Plan a Mystery at Bank of America," *USA Today*, December 11, 2009.
3. Louise Story, "Bank of America Chief Ousted as Chairman," *New York Times*, April 29, 2009, B1.
4. Deborah Jacobs, *How McDonald's Plans Ahead* (Los Angeles: Korn/Ferry Briefings on Talent Leadership, 2011).
5. Eleanor Bloxham, "HP's Next Act," *CNNMoney*, August 10, 2010, <http://money.cnn.com/2010/08/10/technology/HP_post_Hurd_board.fortune/index.htm>.
6. Aaron Ricadela, Carol Hymowitz and Jeffrey McCracken, "HP's Board Is Said to Weigh Ousting Apotheker After Less Than Year as CEO," *Bloomberg*, September 21, 2011.
7. Larry Light and Joan Kiddon,"Brand Revitalization: Background to the Turnaround at McDonald's, *Financial Times*, February 18, 2009.
8. Alan Wilson, interviewed by RHR, 2009.
9. Dennis Zeleny, "Success—And Succession—Takes Planning," *Forbes*, July 19, 2007.
10. David F. Larcker and Brian Tayan, CEO Health Disclosure at Apple: A Public or Private Matter? (Case, Stanford Graduate School of Business, 2011).
11. Booz Allen Hamilton, CEO Succession Survey 2010.
12. Deborah Jacobs, How McDonald's Plans Ahead (Los Angeles: Korn/Ferry Briefings on Talent Leadership, 2011).

## Chapter Eight

1. Warren G. Bennis and Burt Nanus, *Leaders: The Strategies for Taking Charge* (New York: HarperBusiness, 1997).
2. Michael Liedtke, "Yahoo! Fires CEO Carol Bartz, Names CFO as Interim Leader," *Herald-Tribune*, September 7, 2011, <http://www.heraldtribune.com/article/20110907/article/110909714>.

3. Brad Stone and Douglas MacMillan, "Carol Bartz Fired as Yahoo CEO Amid Plans for Strategic Review," *Businessweek*, September 6, 2011.
4. David Goldman, "HP CEO Apotheker Fired, Replaced by Meg Whitman," *CNNMoney*, September 22, 2011, <http://money.cnn.com/2011/09/22/technology/hp_ceo_fired/index.htm>.
5. Ben Worthen and Joann S. Lublin, "Crisis Unfolds at HP Over CEO," *Wall Street Journal*, September 22, 2011.
6. Noel Randewich, "Shares of AMD Slump Following CEO's Departure," *Reuters*, January 11, 2011, <http://www.reuters.com/article/2011/01/11/idUSN1112593620110111>.
7. Agam Shaw, "New AMD CEO Faces Challenges in Mobile," *PC World*, August 2011.
8. Anton Gonsalves, "Acer CEO Resigns Over Board Disagreements," *Information Week*, April 1, 2011.
9. Lorraine Luk, "Acer CEO Resigns as Tablets Threaten Market," *Wall Street Journal*, April 1, 2011.
10. Peter Fasolo, interviewed by RHR, 2009.

## Chapter Nine

1. As Martin Luther King prepared for the Birmingham Campaign in early 1963, he drafted the final sermons for *Strength to Love*, a volume of his most well-known homilies that would be published later that year by HarperCollins. Those final sermons included this quote.
2. "Hay Group/*Chief Executive* survey, *Best Companies for Leaders* (2009).
3. "Phil Condit: Boeing," *Businessweek Online* (January 12, 2004)
4. Bethany McLean and Joe Nocera, *All the Devils Are Here: the Hidden History of the Financial Crisis* (New York: Portfolio/Penguin, 2011).
5. Alec Klein, *Stealing Time: Steve Case, Jerry Levin, and the Collapse of AOL Time Warner* (New York: Simon & Schuster, 2003).
6. Richard A. Davis, *The Intangibles of Leadership: The Ten Qualities of Superior Executive Performance* (San Francisco: Jossey Bass, 2010).
7. John Hanson, interviewed by RHR, 2009.
8. Ciel S. Cantoria, "J&J Embarks on Two-Pronged Succession Planning Program," *Financial Express*, September 27, 2002.
9. Robert P. Gandossy and Nidhi Verma, "Passing the Torch of Leadership," *Leader to Leader* 2006, no. 40 (Spring, 2006): 37–40.
10. Carol Hymowitz and Sarah Frier, "IBM's Rometty Breaks Ground as 100-Year-Old Company's First Female Leader," *Bloomberg*, October 26, 2011.

## Chapter Ten

1. Jack Welch, "Letter to Share Owners," in *GE 2000 Annual Report*.
2. From "Atomic Education Urged by Einstein", *New York Times* (25 May 1946), and later quoted in the article "The Real Problem is in the Hearts

of Man" by Michael Amrine, from the *New York Times Magazine* (23 June 1946). A slightly modified version of the 23 June article was reprinted in *Einstein on Peace* by Otto Nathan and Heinz Norden (1960), and it was also reprinted in *Einstein on Politics* by David E. Rowe and Robert Schulmann (2007), p. 383.

In *The New Quotable Einstein* (2005), editor Alice Calaprice suggests that two quotes attributed to Einstein which she could not find sources for, "The significant problems we face cannot be solved at the same level of thinking we were at when we created them" and "The world we have created today as a result of our thinking thus far has problems which cannot be solved by thinking the way we thought when we created them," may both be paraphrases of the 1946 quote above. A similar unsourced variant is "The world we have created is a product of our thinking; it cannot be changed without changing our thinking."

3. "Ford Names New CEO," *CNNMoney,* September 5, 2006, <http://money.cnn.com/2006/09/05/news/companies/ford/index.htm>.

4. Michael Kanellos and John G. Spooner, "IBM's Outsider: A Look Back at Lou," *CNET,* February 1, 2002, <http://news.cnet.com/2100-1001-828095.html>.

5. Dr. Harry Ashenhurst, interviewed by RHR, 2009.

6. Joseph L. Bower, *The CEO Within: Why Insider Outsiders Are the Key to Succession Planning* (Boston: Harvard Business School Press, 2007).

7. Robert Stein, interviewed by RHR, 2009

8. Bower, *The CEO Within.*

9. "Why Your Next CEO Should Come from Inside," Strategy + Business, December 11, 2007, <http://www.strategy-business.com/article/li00055?pg=all>.

10. "P&G: New and Improved: How A.G. Lafley Is Revolutionizing a Bastion of Corporate Conservatism," *Businessweek*, (July 7, 2003).

11. Matt Richtel, "A Gerstner Loyalist Cut From Quite Different Style," *The New York Times*, January 30, 2002.

## Chapter Eleven

1. RHR/*Chief Executive* joint survey of 236 board directors (2009).

2. RHR International, *Chief Executive Officer Winning Formula, Sample Report*

3. James B. Stewart, "Voting to Hire a Chief Without Meeting Him," *New York Times*, September 21, 2011, B1.

4. Stephen Patrick, interviewed by RHR, 2009.

## Chapter Twelve

1. Booz Allen Hamilton, *CEO Succession Survey 2010.*

2. *Corporate Board Member*/RHR International, *Transitions In Leadership* (Brentwood, TN: *Corporate Board Member*/RHR International, 2011).

3. *Corporate Board Member*/RHR International, *Transitions In Leadership* (Brentwood, TN: *Corporate Board Member*/RHR International, 2011).
4. George Brandt, "Why Preparing in Advance is Priceless: How MasterCard CEO Ajay Banga Planned Ahead for His New Leadership Role," *Forbes*, February 23 2011.
5. Andrew Martin, "Avon Announces Plans to Name a New Chief Executive," *New York Times*, December 13, 2011, B2.
6. Hannah Karp and Joann S. Lublin, "Former CEOs Criticize Avon," *Wall Street Journal*, December 22, 2011.
7. Andrew Martin, "Avon Announces Plans to Name a New Chief Executive," *New York Times*, December 13, 2011, B2.
8. RHR/*Chief Executive* joint survey of 236 board directors (2009)
9. Thomas Neff and James Citrin, *You're in Charge—Now What? : The 8 Point Plan* (New York: Crown Business, 2005).
10. RHR International, *Executive Selection and Integration: Beyond the First 90 Days* (Chicago: RHR International Research, 2005).

## Chapter Thirteen

1. Peter F. Drucker, "What Makes an Effective Executive," *Harvard Business Review*, (June 2004), 58.
2. George Santayana, *The Life of Reason* (New York: Charles Scribner's Sons, 1905).
3. *Corporate Board Member*/RHR International, *Transitions In Leadership* (Brentwood, TN: *Corporate Board Member*/RHR International, 2011).
4. David Mildenberg, "Bank of America's Lewis Resigns After Bet on Rebound," *Bloomberg*, October 1, 2009.
5. E. Scott Reckard, "Bank of America Names Brian Monyihan As New Chief Executive," *Los Angeles Times*, December 17, 2009.

## Chapter Fourteen

1. Henry Ford with Samuel Crowther, *My Life and Work* (Whitefish, MT: Kessinger Publishing, 2003).

## Epilogue

1. U.S. Census Bureau (2012).
2. John Hamre, Center for Strategic and International Studies, Washington D.C., Chicago Council on Global Affairs, Board Retreat, (2006).
3. Kent Greenes and Diane Piktalis, *Bridging the Gaps: How to Transfer Knowledge in Today's Multigenerational Workplace* (Ottawa: The Conference Board, 2008).
4. Ram Charan, "Ending the CEO Succession Crisis," *Harvard Business Review*, (February 2005).

5. Booz Allen Hamilton, *CEO Succession Survey 2010*.
6. U.S. Department of Labor & Statistics (2010).
7. Grant Thornton International Business Report (2010).
8. Dr. Roy D Adler, *Women in the Executive Suite Correlate to High Profits* (Glass Ceiling Research Center, 2001).
9. Antoine van Agtmael, *The Emerging Markets Century: How a New Breed of World-Class Companies Is Overtaking the World* (New York: Free Press, 2007).

# INDEX